The Medieval Crusades

Stephen Currie

LUCENT BOOKS
A part of Gale, Cengage Learning

Detroit • New York • San Francisco • New Haven, Conn • Waterville, Maine • London

GALE
CENGAGE Learning™

LIBRARY OF CONGRESS CATALOGING-IN-PUBLICATION DATA

Currie, Stephen.
  The Medieval crusades / by Stephen Currie.
    p. cm. -- (World history)
  Includes bibliographical references and index.
  ISBN 978-1-4205-0062-2 (hardcover)
  1. Crusades--Juvenile literature. 2. Civilization, Medieval--Juvenile literature. I. Title.
  D157.C87 2009
  909.07--dc22
                                                    2008046532

Lucent Books
27500 Drake Rd.
Farmington Hills, MI 48331

ISBN-13: 978-1-4205-0062-2
ISBN-10: 1-4205-0062-7

Printed in the United States of America
1 2 3 4 5 6 7 13 12 11 10 09

Contents

Foreword

Each year, on the first day of school, nearly every history teacher faces the task of explaining why his or her students should study history. Many reasons have been given. One is that lessons exist in the past from which contemporary society can benefit and learn. Another is that exploration of the past allows us to see the origins of our customs, ideas, and institutions. Concepts such as democracy, ethnic conflict, or even things as trivial as fashion or mores, have historical roots.

Reasons such as these impress few students, however. If anything, these explanations seem remote and dull to young minds. Yet history is anything but dull. And therein lies what is perhaps the most compelling reason for studying history: History is filled with great stories. The classic themes of literature and drama—love and sacrifice, hatred and revenge, injustice and betrayal, adversity and overcoming adversity—fill the pages of history books, feeding the imagination as well as any of the great works of fiction do.

The story of the Children's Crusade, for example, is one of the most tragic in history. In 1212 Crusader fever hit Europe. A call went out from the pope that all good Christians should journey to Jerusalem to drive out the hated Muslims and return the city to Christian control. Heeding the call, thousands of children made the journey. Parents bravely allowed many children to go, and entire communities were inspired by the faith of these small Crusaders. Unfortunately, many boarded ships captained by slave traders, who enthusiastically sold the children into slavery as soon as they arrived at their destination. Thousands died from disease, exposure, and starvation on the long march across Europe to the Mediterranean Sea. Others perished at sea.

Another story, from a modern and more familiar place, offers a soul-wrenching view of personal humiliation but also the ability to rise above it. Hatsuye Egami was one of 110,000 Japanese Americans sent to internment camps during World War II. "Since yesterday we Japanese have ceased to be human beings," he wrote in his diary. "We are numbers. We are no longer Egamis, but the number 23324. A tag with that number is on every trunk, suitcase and bag. Tags, also, on our breasts." Despite such dehumanizing treatment, most internees worked hard to control their bitterness. They created workable communities inside the camps and demonstrated again and again their loyalty as Americans.

These are but two of the many stories from history that can be found in the pages of the Lucent Books World History series. All World History titles rely on sound research and verifiable evidence, and all give students a clear sense of time, place, and chronology through maps and timelines as well as text.

All titles include a wide range of authoritative perspectives that demonstrate the complexity of historical interpretation and sharpen the reader's critical thinking skills. Formally documented quotations and annotated bibliographies enable students to locate and evaluate sources, often instantaneously via the Internet, and serve as valuable tools for further research and debate.

Finally, Lucent's World History titles present rousing good stories, featuring vivid primary source quotations drawn from unique, sometimes obscure sources such as diaries, public records, and contemporary chronicles. In this way, the voices of participants and witnesses as well as important biographers and historians bring the study of history to life. As we are caught up in the lives of others, we are reminded that we too are characters in the ongoing human saga, and we are better prepared for our own roles.

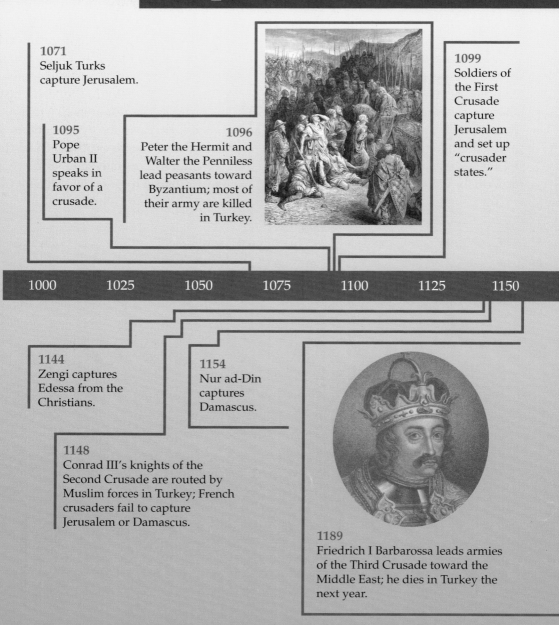

1071
Seljuk Turks capture Jerusalem.

1095
Pope Urban II speaks in favor of a crusade.

1096
Peter the Hermit and Walter the Penniless lead peasants toward Byzantium; most of their army are killed in Turkey.

1099
Soldiers of the First Crusade capture Jerusalem and set up "crusader states."

| 1000 | 1025 | 1050 | 1075 | 1100 | 1125 | 1150 |

1144
Zengi captures Edessa from the Christians.

1154
Nur ad-Din captures Damascus.

1148
Conrad III's knights of the Second Crusade are routed by Muslim forces in Turkey; French crusaders fail to capture Jerusalem or Damascus.

1189
Friedrich I Barbarossa leads armies of the Third Crusade toward the Middle East; he dies in Turkey the next year.

of the Medieval Crusades

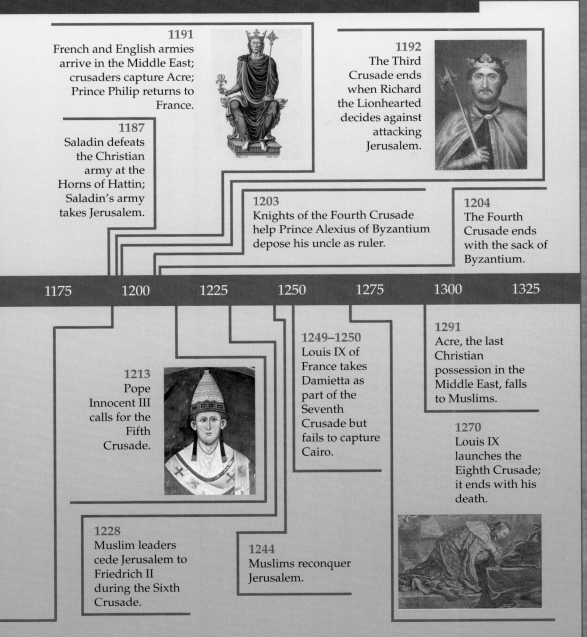

1191
French and English armies arrive in the Middle East; crusaders capture Acre; Prince Philip returns to France.

1192
The Third Crusade ends when Richard the Lionhearted decides against attacking Jerusalem.

1187
Saladin defeats the Christian army at the Horns of Hattin; Saladin's army takes Jerusalem.

1203
Knights of the Fourth Crusade help Prince Alexius of Byzantium depose his uncle as ruler.

1204
The Fourth Crusade ends with the sack of Byzantium.

1175   1200   1225   1250   1275   1300   1325

1291
Acre, the last Christian possession in the Middle East, falls to Muslims.

1213
Pope Innocent III calls for the Fifth Crusade.

1249–1250
Louis IX of France takes Damietta as part of the Seventh Crusade but fails to capture Cairo.

1270
Louis IX launches the Eighth Crusade; it ends with his death.

1228
Muslim leaders cede Jerusalem to Friedrich II during the Sixth Crusade.

1244
Muslims reconquer Jerusalem.

The Crusades

The Crusades were a series of wars that stretched from the late 1000s to the end of the 1200s and took place in and around the Middle East, especially in present-day Turkey, Syria, Israel, and Egypt. In general, the Crusades pitted the Christians of western Europe against the Muslims of the Middle East. However, the Byzantine Christians of eastern Europe and the Middle East were often involved as well. Sometimes they stood with the Christians of the West, and sometimes they fought against them.

On one level, the Crusades were fought over matters of religion. Indeed, the word *crusade* implies a holy journey of conquest. The battles were fought primarily over territories that had sacred meaning. In addition, Muslims and Christians were often quick to condemn the teachings and rituals of the other faith. For both Muslims and Christians, then, the Crusades were an attempt to gain the upper hand over those who believed in a foreign and objectionable religion. Both sides referred to their opponents as infidels, or unbelievers.

At the same time, though, religion was only part of the reason behind the Crusades. Just as important were political, social, and economic concerns. Muslim control of Christian holy lands was unacceptable to Christians not only because Islam seemed an alien religion, but also because the growing military power of the Muslims threatened the influence and stability of the Christian kingdoms nearby. Crusaders from western Europe fought in part to line their pockets with Eastern treasures. Furthermore, the Crusades helped bring Christian groups together in opposition to a common enemy. While religious fervor played an enormous role in the Crusades, then, there were other motives for the fighting as well.

Romance and Reality

In the popular imagination of the modern era, the Crusades were a time of courage, glory, and romance. Movies about the Crusades often show handsome Christian knights in bright white clothing with bold red crosses on their chests. Among Westerners, the men who led the Christian attackers are remembered as brave and heroic. The same is true in Muslim countries, though the situation is reversed: For Muslims, the heroes of the Crusades were the ancestors of today's Middle Easterners, who defended themselves and their religion against the attacks of outsiders.

As is often true of wars, however, the reality of the Crusades is a good deal less glamorous and romantic than many believe. Splendid uniforms were the exception, not the rule, and cleanliness was almost impossible to maintain. Many soldiers on both sides had inadequate supplies, and they died by the hundreds from hunger, illness, and exhaustion, as well as from wounds received in battle.

Nor was the war a struggle between two principled enemies who treated prisoners well and avoided bringing violence to nonparticipants. On the contrary, the religious nature of the conflict convinced both sides that any action taken in defense of their faith was acceptable. Thus, both sides, but particularly the Christians, plundered cities, massacred townspeople, and destroyed property.

The Crusades had an important impact on history, partly because of all this violence and brutality. The Crusades resulted

The Crusades were a series of wars that took place in and around the Middle East and lasted from the late 1000s to the end of the 1200s.

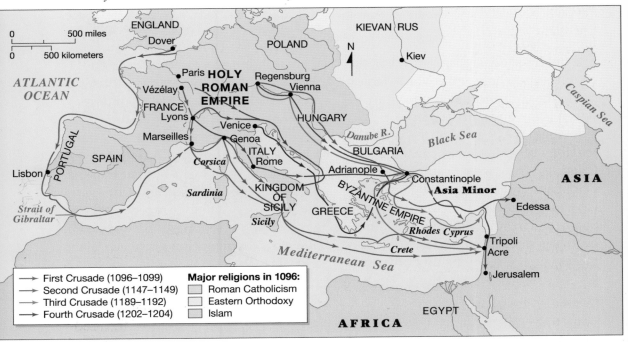

in the deaths of thousands and thousands of people, soldiers and civilians alike. The wars displaced thousands more, forcing them from their homes and taking away their livelihoods. The Crusades sparked Europeans' curiosity about the rest of the world, indirectly leading to the increased trade of the Renaissance era and the voyages of exploration led by Christopher Columbus and others. The Muslims, in the long run, strengthened their religious and political hold on the Middle East.

Islam and Christianity

The longest-lasting effect of the Crusades, however, was on the relationship between Christians and Muslims. Even today, the tensions between these two groups can be extremely high. Not all Muslims view Christianity with suspicion, of course, and neither do all Christians mistrust Islam as a whole. Still, the terrorist attacks of September 11, 2001, the U.S.-led invasion of predominantly Muslim Iraq and Afghanistan, and other conflicts elsewhere in the world demonstrate the complicated connections between Islam and Christianity.

It would not be accurate to say that the tensions of today were caused by the Crusades. There were hostilities between Christians and Muslims long before the Crusades began—in the Middle East, in Spain, and in other places as well. In the centuries since the end of the Crusades, moreover, the relationship between Islam and Christianity has sometimes been quite positive. Clearly, the violence of the Crusades did not pit Christian against Muslim on any kind of permanent basis.

Still, though the Crusades did not create today's conflicts, they did play a role in shaping them. For two centuries, after all, the Muslims of the Middle East and the Christians of western Europe were frequently at war. Nor was the war an ordinary war over land or trade; it was in part a holy war in which both sides were convinced that they were in the right. Each side used the injustices committed against them to rally their troops as well as to "prove" that the enemy was heartless and inhuman. Indeed, the level of anger and hatred during the Crusades was enormous; many soldiers on each side fervently hoped to wipe the enemy off the face of the earth.

The battles of the Crusades left scars and bruises on the bodies of the soldiers, but perhaps even more important, these wars also left scars and bruises on the memories and in the hearts of Muslims and Christians alike. These wounds may have lessened with time, but they have never fully disappeared. Generations later, it is still possible to see the anger, fear, and mutual mistrust that marked the dealings of Muslims and Christians during the Crusades. Even today, the old wounds of these long-gone wars continue to color interactions between Islam and Christianity.

Chapter One

Europe and the Middle East

The Crusades did not begin until close to the year 1100. The roots of the conflict between Christian Europeans and Middle Eastern Muslims, however, go back hundreds of years before that. There had been political struggles for years between various groups in the Middle East, for example, and these helped create an atmosphere in which the Crusades could take place. The details of religious doctrines and practices were likewise important in creating the divides between the warring groups. Other events played a role as well. In order to understand the Crusades, it is first necessary to understand the world that produced them.

Christianity

In a sense, the story of the Crusades begins with the development of Christianity in the years before A.D. 100. Christianity grew out of Judaism, a long-established faith in the Middle East, and it centered on the Jew-

ish prophet Jesus. To Christians, Jesus was the son of God, part human and part divine. According to Christians, Jesus voluntarily submitted to death by crucifixion—that is, by being nailed to a cross—to atone for all the sins committed by ordinary humans. Moreover, Jesus quickly came back to life. His triumph over death represented the triumph of God's great love over the powers of evil and offered believers hope of eternal life in heaven.

Christianity was very much a fringe religion in its earliest years, and its long-term survival was in doubt. Many rulers and religious leaders in and around the Middle East disapproved of it. Some persecuted those who tried to practice the Christian faith, and a few attempted to ban the religion altogether. The powerful Roman Empire, which controlled much of the area around the Mediterranean Sea, was especially suspicious of Christianity. Roman leaders saw Christianity's spiritual

The roots of the Crusades lay partly in the development of Christianity, which centered on the Jewish prophet Jesus. Leaders and rulers in the Middle East, as well as in the powerful Roman Empire, disapproved of Christianity. Nevertheless, Christianity flourished and quickly spread to nations all over the world.

ideas as a challenge to the traditional religious practices common throughout the empire. Despite the hostility it attracted, however, Christianity did not die. On the contrary, it began gaining converts in Greece, North Africa, and elsewhere. By A.D. 300 there were many thousands of Christians living throughout the Mediterranean region.

Further growth was still to come. In 313, with the support of the Roman emperor Constantine—who some say converted to Christianity himself toward the end of his life—the empire dropped all penalties against those who practiced the new faith. No longer required to be secretive, Christians became a force in public life, and the number of Christians sharply increased. In 395 the empire went even further. Under the leadership of the openly Christian emperor Theodosius, Rome adopted Christianity as the official state religion. Even when the Roman Empire collapsed a few years later, Christianity continued to flourish. Before long, it had spread to nations as distant and diverse as England in Europe, Armenia in Asia, and Ethiopia in eastern Africa.

Byzantium and Rome

Despite the rapid increase in numbers and influence, however, the Christian world was not unified. From early on there were two main centers of Christian activity, each based in a large and powerful city near the Mediterranean Sea. One was the city of Byzantium, also called Constantinople, which sat on the border between Asia and Europe. Today this city is known as Istanbul, Turkey.

The other was Rome, the capital of the former Roman Empire. For the most part, Christians in western Europe looked to Rome for guidance, and Christians in eastern Europe and elsewhere looked to Byzantium.

The Christian authorities in the two cities, however, did not see eye to eye. Their religious and cultural practices were not the same. The Byzantine churches used Greek as their primary language, for example, and the Roman churches used Latin. The churches could not agree on the origin of the Holy Spirit, one manifestation of the divine. Leaders quarreled incessantly, moreover, over the question of who had greater authority—the Roman pope, the head of the western branch, or the patriarch of Byzantium, who led the eastern.

The cities viewed themselves in very different ways, too. Byzantium was a refined city that valued learning and art. As capital of the large and powerful Byzantine Empire, it had extensive political influence in addition to being an important spiritual hub. It was also among the wealthiest and most imposing cities of its time. As one deeply impressed western European put it, "Never had so grand an enterprise been carried out by any people since the creation of the world."[1]

Rome, in contrast, was—in the words of historian Steven Runciman—"a paltry city."[2] With the collapse of the Roman Empire in the early 400s, Rome had lost a good deal of its sophistication and prosperity. By 1000 it produced little of much value to the rest of the world; it was technologically and educationally backward; it impressed few visitors. Rome had also lost its political strength. Although western Europeans were willing to recognize Rome's authority in religious matters, they did not typically follow Rome's lead where politics were concerned.

For that matter, no political authority seemed able to unify the people of western Europe. With the one exception of religion, the Christians of western Europe were sharply divided in almost every conceivable way. They looked with deep suspicion on people who belonged to other ethnic groups, came from different regions, or spoke different languages. Partly as a result, they fought their neighbors frequently. Indeed, the history of western Europe in the years before the Crusades is in large part the story of innumerable wars fought between neighboring peoples, all or nearly all of them Christian. As the year 1000 approached, then, Byzantium seemed solid, important, and secure. Rome, in contrast, was none of those things.

The Great Schism

In the early 1000s, the disagreements between Rome and Byzantium became increasingly bitter. In 1054 envoys from both cities met in Byzantium to discuss the differences between them. The meeting, however, did not go well. The envoys could not come to a compromise. At last, Cardinal Humbert, the leader of the Roman delegates, acted; he excommunicated the patriarch of Byzantium. That is, he declared that the patriarch was no longer a member of the church.

The patriarch responded, not surprisingly, by excommunicating Humbert.

These double excommunications led to the Great Schism, a formal split between the eastern and western branches of Christianity. Essentially, Romans and Byzantines gave up on the idea of complete unity. Roman leaders continued to recognize the Byzantines as Christians, if misguided, and did not necessarily consider them enemies; the reverse held true as well. However, neither side accepted the authority of church leaders in the other city. For centuries, the church had held together despite areas of significant disagreement. Now, though, there was no longer one Christian church— there were two.

Islam

The differences between the western and eastern churches were made more complex by the presence of another powerful religion in the Middle East. This was Islam. Islam, which developed on the Arabian Peninsula in the early 600s, has much in common with both Judaism and Christianity. All three faiths accept the Hebrew Bible as a sacred text and see themselves as descended from the Old Testament figure of Abraham. Indeed, the three faiths are often known as the Abrahamic religions or "People of the Book," with "the Book" being the Hebrew Bible. Muslims, again like Christians and Jews, believe in one god, known as Allah in the Islamic faith. Likewise, all three faiths value prayer, charitable giving, and several other actions with spiritual significance.

بنا بی مسجد کلدی کندو قاعده سنجه اورو طوردی

Muhammad founded Islam and is considered to be the greatest of the prophets. In this painting, Muhammad delivers his last sermon.

The religions also have substantial differences, however. Islam was founded by a man named Muhammad. To Muslims, Muhammad is a prophet, or a person who speaks spiritual truths; in fact, he is considered the greatest of the prophets, a messenger sent from God to the people of the world. In contrast, Muhammad plays no role in either Judaism or Christianity. Islam's main sacred text is the Koran, which again has no particular meaning to the other Abrahamic faiths. Furthermore, Islam includes many practices and doctrines unfamiliar to Christians. For instance, Muslims are expected to make a journey to the holy city of Mecca at least once in their lives, and they celebrate holidays that do not appear in the calendars of the other religions.

Islam grew quickly. By the mid-600s most of the Arabian Peninsula had been converted to the new religion. By 750 there were Muslims through most of the Middle East and the northern strip of Africa; Islam had also made its way into Spain on the west and as far east as present-day Pakistan. As with Christianity, not all Muslims practiced their religion the same way. Muslims were divided into two main groups, the Sunnis and the Shiites, each with its own religious ideas and customs. Muslims, like the people of western Europe, also split along ethnic lines. Thus, there was plenty of fighting among various Muslim groups for whom ethnic differences outweighed religious similarities.

Coexistence

Christianity and Islam had little contact during the early 600s, when Muslims lived almost exclusively on the Arabian Peninsula. As Islam spread, however, the

followers of the two religions came together more and more. In some places, Christians and Muslims got along well. The Middle Eastern city of Jerusalem was a good example. Jerusalem was the holiest city in Christianity, just as Mecca was to Muslims. In the early 600s, at the time that Muhammad founded Islam, Jerusalem was controlled by Christians. Thousands of Christians lived in and around the city. Many Christians who did not live nearby made sacred journeys, or pilgrimages, to Jerusalem.

In 638, however, as part of ongoing warfare between the various peoples of the Middle East, Muslims captured the city and the surrounding areas. They could have forced the Christians to leave, but they did not. Moreover, they opened the gates of the city to Jews, who had been excluded under Christian rule. As

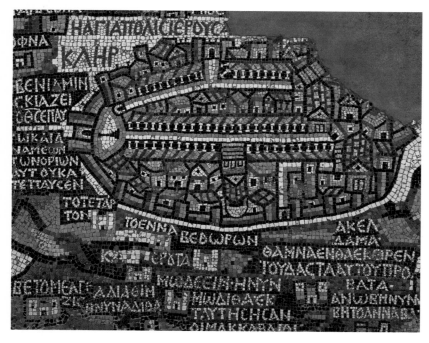

During the 600s Jerusalem, shown here as a mosaic, was a place where Christians, Jews, and Muslims lived harmoniously. The three groups had certain spiritual and cultural similarities, which allowed them to coexist in relative peace.

Peace and War

Both Islam and Christianity have long had complex teachings about war. Islam often considers itself to be a religion of peace, and indeed Muslims have had many peaceful and tolerant relationships with people of other religions over time. Yet Islam also has the doctrine of jihad, or holy war. This concept does not require believers to go to war against those of other faiths; but it does help justify attacks against people who are not themselves Muslim. Thus, Islam both supports and opposes warfare.

The same is true of Christianity. Jesus counseled that people should turn the other cheek when injured, rather than responding with violence, and for many Christians a desire to make and preserve peace is central to their faith. At the same time, the Bible also describes various acts of brutality with evident approval, and most Christian thinkers do not feel that pacifism is always appropriate. The uncertain status of war in both religions allowed rulers on both sides to accept and encourage warfare as part of the Crusades.

a result, Christians, Jews, and Muslims all lived together in Jerusalem for the next several centuries. The three groups maintained their separate identities, and there were certainly periods of unrest between people of different faiths. Still, as historian Michael Foss describes it, the people of Jerusalem, whatever their background, "rubb[ed] together peacefully enough."[3] The Muslims allowed the Christian tradition of pilgrimage to continue as well.

Part of the reason for this tolerance was the fact that Judaism, Islam, and Christianity not only shared spiritual texts and doctrines, but they held many cultural features in common, too. The different faiths sprang up in the same part of the world, after all, and among peoples whose ways of life were much alike.

In particular, eastern Christians and the Muslims of the Middle East shared important characteristics and recognized the achievements of each others' civilizations. To a degree, in fact, eastern Christians were more closely connected to urban Muslims than they were to the Christians of western Europe. According to Steven Runciman, the people of Byzantium, in the years before the Crusades, "would have felt far more at home in Cairo or Baghdad than in Paris or Aachen [a city in what is now Germany] or even Rome."[4]

Strife

But although Muslims and Christians coexisted peacefully in parts of the world, that was not the case everywhere. There was scattered warfare in the Middle East, especially on the fringes of the Byzantine Empire. Moreover, there were strong tensions in western and southern Europe. Muslim leaders had conquered Spain and Portugal in the early 700s, much to the dismay of Christian officials in Rome. The Italian island of Sicily fell to the Muslims as well, and Muslim pirates threatened sailors all through the Mediterranean Sea. In 846 some Muslim raiders attacked Rome itself and carried off some of its religious treasures.

Then, in the very early 1000s, relations between Christians and Muslims started to deteriorate even in places where they had been reasonably good. The troubles began when a new Muslim leader, Abu Ali al-Mansur al-Hakim bi-Amrih Allah, took control of Jerusalem and the surrounding areas. Al-Hakim reversed the religious tolerance that had marked Jerusalem for so many centuries. As a historian writes, "He ordered Jews and Christians to wear sashes around their waists and badges on their clothes. Christians dressed in black and hung great wooden crosses around their necks, the length of a forearm and weighing much."[5] Al-Hakim ordered the destruction of many Christian churches, too.

Al-Hakim disappeared into the desert under mysterious circumstances in 1021. The status of Christians rose somewhat under his successors, and some of the churches were rebuilt. As one Muslim described the biggest of these churches, "I saw seated in this church great numbers of priests and monks, reading the Scriptures and saying prayers, both by day and night."[6] Still, all was not as it had been before. The reign of al-Hakim had unnerved Christians of the region. The

Strong tensions existed between the Muslims and Christians in western and southern Europe. In this painting, Muslims capture the Byzantine city of Messina in Sicily.

The Jews and the World in 1000

The Jews were the first of the three People of the Book. Their origins go back long before the birth of Jesus or the works of Muhammad. Yet by the time of the Crusades, they were the least powerful of the three Abrahamic religions. In 1000 some Jews lived in the Middle East, where for the most part they were tolerated—if not necessarily liked—by the Muslims who governed the region. Others had migrated to Europe. Some of these had traveled to western Europe, especially Germany, France, and Spain.

The status of these European Jews varied considerably, both by place and by time. In parts of Spain, in particular, they were treated quite well, but in parts of Germany and especially in France, Jews were often oppressed. They had few rights; laws limited where they could live, what jobs they could hold, and where they could go. Moreover, in times of stress, such as during famines or outbreaks of disease, even relatively tolerant populations often took out their frustrations on the local Jews. Wherever they traveled during the era of the Crusades, Jews could never feel completely safe.

situation grew even less comfortable later in the century, when Jerusalem's leaders began levying extra taxes on Christian pilgrims who wished to travel to the region—and when bands of Muslims north of Jerusalem began attacking the pilgrims and robbing them.

The Seljuk Turks

At about the same time, the rulers of Byzantium grew worried about another Muslim group, known as the Seljuk Turks. The Seljuk Turks originated in central Asia, but during the 1000s they began moving westward, conquering other peoples as they traveled. Before long, they controlled large sections of territory south and east of Byzantium. The Seljuk Turks were quite powerful—and they were unified in a way that other Muslim groups in the area were not. The Byzantines were concerned that the Seljuk Turks would take parts of their empire—and perhaps, someday, attack Byzantium itself.

These worries grew stronger in 1071, when the Seljuk Turks captured Jerusalem. On the surface, nothing had changed; the city had been in Muslim hands before the Seljuk victory, and it was still Muslim property. The Seljuk Turks presented a more serious threat to the Byzantines than the previous Muslims, however, and the Seljuks now began to push farther west and north. Over the next few years,

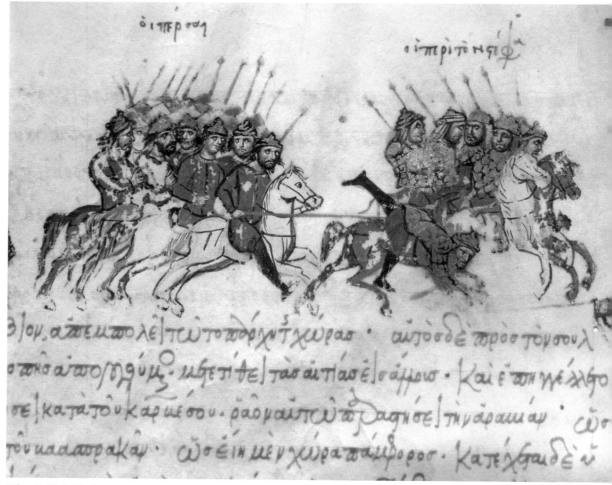

The Seljuk Turks were a powerful Muslim group that posed a serious threat to the Byzantines. They captured Jerusalem in 1071 and attempted to conquer Byzantium.

Seljuk armies steadily gained new territory. By 1080 most of present-day Turkey was under Seljuk control, and the Seljuk soldiers were closing in on Byzantium itself.

Byzantine soldiers were able to rally before the Seljuks could reach the city, and they managed to stop the advancing Muslims about 100 miles (160 km) east of Byzantium. Over the next few years, the two sides skirmished on several occasions without the Seljuks coming any closer. Still, the danger to Byzantium persisted. And there were other troubling issues, too. In a reversal of earlier policy, the Seljuks had stopped permitting Christian pilgrims to enter Jerusalem. There were reports, moreover, that Christians in the Holy Land were being oppressed under Seljuk rule.

In 1095 Byzantium's emperor, Alexius I Comnenus, decided to rid the region of the Seljuk menace once and for all. He hoped to push the Seljuks out of present-day Turkey and regain control of Jerusalem and the Holy Land. In the process, he would reestablish Byzantium as the dominant power in the area. The war, as Alexius saw it, would be a holy crusade, a righteous struggle with an impact far beyond that of an ordinary conflict. In his eyes, the war would pit good against evil, the true faith of Christianity against the error of Islam, the forces of light against the forces of darkness.

It was a dramatic plan, and it would have equally dramatic consequences. Without knowing it, Alexius was setting into motion forces that neither he, nor anyone else, could possibly control.

Chapter Two

The First Crusade

Alexius did not immediately begin his campaign to bring Jerusalem and the Holy Land back under Christian control. He feared that his army might not be strong enough to defeat the powerful Seljuks. Accordingly, he looked to Rome for support. Alexius, of course, was well aware of the feuds between his church and the church of western Europe. Nonetheless, Alexius hoped that the Westerners would come to his aid. He believed that their shared identity as Christians would prove stronger than the differences that kept them apart.

Pope Urban II

In 1095 Alexius sent a group of ambassadors to a meeting of western Christian leaders in Rome. The ambassadors spoke to the assembled churchmen, including Pope Urban II. They outlined Alexius's plans and requested military assistance. Urban immediately pressured the other church leaders to agree. Deeply con-cerned for the future of Christianity, Urban believed that Christians had a moral duty to fight the Muslims, to reclaim the Holy Land, and to establish the dominance of their faith. On a more worldly level, he also hoped to divert the energies of Europe's knights away from attacking one another and toward attacking a common foe instead.

In November 1095, Urban gave a speech in which he described the situation in the Middle East. The Holy Land, he said, had been overrun by Muslims, "an accursed race, a race wholly alienated from God."[7] These "accursed" Muslims were doing their best to interfere with the practice of Christianity. The persecution of Middle Eastern Christians, the closing of Jerusalem to pilgrims, the spread of the Seljuks toward Byzantium—all were terrible wrongs, Urban explained.

As Urban saw it, there was just one way to right the wrongs, and that was through violence. He instructed Chris-

Pope Urban II urged Christians to provide military assistance against the Muslims in order to reclaim Jerusalem and to help establish Christianity as the dominant faith.

tians to form a massive army that would sweep down on the Muslim enemy and defeat the menace once and for all. He explained that Christians had a solemn obligation to defend other Christians and to fight for their religion. "I call on those present here. I proclaim it to the absent," Urban said, and then he backed up his statements with the voice of authority: "Moreover, Christ commands it."[8]

Furthermore, in case the words of the pope and Jesus himself were not enough, Urban added another incentive for men to join the fighting force. "If those who set out thither [to the Middle East] should lose their lives on the way by land, or in crossing the sea, or in fighting the pagans," he promised, "their sins shall be remitted."[9] That is, they would be forgiven for any evil they had ever done and would be allowed to enter heaven immediately upon their deaths. According to the standard theology of the time, only a small percentage of Christians would ever reach heaven. For a people that believed absolutely in heaven and hell, the pope's promise was quite appealing.

In addition to promising heaven to those who did his bidding, Urban also issued threats to those who chose not to go. "What reproaches will be charged against you by the Lord Himself if you have not helped those who are counted, like yourselves, of the Christian faith!"[10] he cautioned. Urban exempted the old and the sick from service but otherwise accepted no excuses for men who failed to fight. Urban pointed out that Jesus once said, "He that loveth father and mother more than me is not worthy of me" (Matthew 10:37), and he insisted that no earthly desires or responsibilities outweighed the call to arms. "Let none of your possessions restrain you," he said, "nor anxiety for your family affairs."[11]

Two Armies

Urban's speech was well received by the people who heard it. The news that an army was forming spread quickly across Europe. Some nobles and knights began putting together an elite fighting force to serve under the guidance of the pope himself. Urban had instructed them to be ready to leave by August 1096, less than a year in the future. Accordingly, these men began selling possessions to raise money for the trek east, and they made plans for the care of their lands and families while they were away.

Urban was quite pleased with the response of these noblemen. His speech had been aimed mainly at the upper classes; he was eager to send Alexius the finest fighters the West could offer. But the speech was equally popular among the lower classes of Europe. Several men, including a monk known as Peter the Hermit and a soldier called Walter the Penniless, repeated Urban's message to ordinary Europeans. They found a willing audience. The life of a peasant was extremely hard, and recent floods, droughts, and famines had only made things worse. A glorious war against the Muslim enemy, with the prospect of heaven for those who died, seemed a better alternative to many of western Europe's poor. In March 1096 Peter and Walter set out for the east with twenty thousand or more men, women, and children, all of them eager to do battle for Christ.

Their mission, however, got off to a problematic start. The assembled soldiers had little sense of military discipline. Some of the troops spent most of the journey looting, damaging property, and occasionally killing the people they passed. The Jews of central Europe were particular targets for this behavior. In the eyes of many of the peasants, there was

Peter the Hermit spreads Pope Urban's message about the First Crusade. Peter and Walter the Penniless, with an army of more than twenty thousand, went willingly into battle against the Muslims.

little difference between the Jews of Europe and the Muslims of the Middle East. Certainly, both were perceived as enemies. "It was as praiseworthy to get rid of one as the other," notes a historian, "and the [Jews were] closest."[12]

As the trip continued, the ragged army began to dwindle. Some died of disease. Others went home. Skirmishes with local people continued, sometimes sparked by the crusaders, other times by the locals; some crusaders died during these battles, and others were taken prisoner. Members of the group quarreled over leadership and planning. Splinter groups broke off to follow different routes. In

August, when the bulk of the peasants reached the gates of Byzantium after a journey of close to 1,500 miles (2,400km), they were exhausted, hungry, and even less presentable than they had been when they left home.

"They Tore Down Palaces"

Alexius was not especially pleased to see the peasants. These travelers were not what he had expected from Urban. They had arrived ahead of schedule, and there were far more of them than he had anticipated. Most important, the army did not consist of the knights and princes Urban had promised. Peter the Hermit explained that the army was ready to fight, but Alexius was unconvinced. He fed and housed the crusaders for a time, trying to keep them busy until the knights and nobles arrived.

The crusaders, however, were not willing to wait. Eager for battle, they turned their aggressions against their hosts. "They tore down palaces in the city," wrote a chronicler of the time, "set fire to public buildings, [and] stripped lead off the churches and sold it." Although they had promised to fight the Muslims, the writer continued, "they everywhere plundered Christians, unrestrained either by the heavy hand of [Alexius] or the fear of God."[13]

Enraged by this behavior, Alexius sent the peasants off toward the Muslim strongholds after all. As he had anticipated, though, the ragtag army was no match for the well-trained Seljuk soldiers. In October the Seljuks and the peasants met in present-day Turkey. The resulting battle was one-sided in the extreme. According to Anna Comnena, Alexius's daughter, the Christians "were wretchedly cut to pieces."[14] Hundreds upon hundreds of crusaders were killed, and others were taken prisoner. The few survivors straggled back into Byzantium. The first campaign of the Crusades was over, and it had not ended well for the Christian attackers.

The Second Wave

The second wave of crusaders was made up of nobles and knights, along with an unknown number of foot soldiers—most of them peasants in the employ of the nobles and the knights. Many of them, though by no means all, were members of an ethnic group called the Franks, relatives of the modern-day French; the crusaders, as a result, were often known simply as the Franks. They took various routes to the east and began trickling into Byzantium in late 1096 and early 1097.

Alexius was pleased to see that this group included the knights that he had expected, but once again he was distressed by how many there were. According to Anna Comnena, the crusaders were "as numerous as the stars of heaven or the grains of sand."[15] Alexius suspected that they intended to seize Jerusalem for Rome, rather than helping Byzantium to reclaim it. Worse, he wondered if the crusaders truly meant to continue on to Jerusalem or if their real aim was the conquest of Byzantium itself. The presence of the Franks made him feel vulnerable.

To forestall a possible attack, Alexius made sure the crusaders saw the size and

Alexius and the Franks

Alexius did not much like most of the crusader knights, but his daughter Anna was intrigued by some of them. She rhapsodized in her journal about several in particular, noticing their height, their bearing, and their good looks. In turn, the Franks held very different impressions of Alexius. A few of the crusader knights greatly admired him. "There is no man today like him under heaven," wrote Stephen of Blois to his wife. "[He] is relieving all our knights with gifts and the poor with feasts."

However, others viewed Alexius with a good deal of suspicion. They were intimidated by his sophistication and worried constantly that he was trying to trick them. At the same time, without noting the inconsistency in these beliefs, they charged that he was a fool who knew nothing and was going to lead the crusaders to certain death. The crusaders' mixed attitudes toward Alexius reflected the general view of the Byzantines among Westerners of the time.

Quoted in August C. Krey, *The First Crusade.* Gloucester, MA: Peter Smith, 1921, p. 100.

The crusaders' opinions of Alexius varied widely, from admiration to deep suspicion.

skill of his own army. He also invited the crusaders' leaders to visit his palace, one by one. As Alexius expected, they were awed by the emperor's wealth and the luxury of his accommodations. Once they were suitably intimidated, Alexius casually asked them to sign a document promising to give the Byzantine Empire control over any former Christian possessions they recaptured in the Holy Land. Some of the Franks signed at once. Others were more cautious. In the end, though, nearly all agreed to the contract.

Still, all was not as Alexius had planned. He had originally hoped to bring the Westerners into his own army to stage an attack

The Journey East

The nobles and knights who made up the second wave of crusaders had a difficult time getting to Byzantium. Many crusaders were assaulted and even killed by hostile locals. Sometimes the locals were trying to keep the large armies out of their villages or thought that the crusaders might be an enemy. Other times, the crusaders began the hostilities by taking villagers' food, looting random houses, or deciding on very little evidence that the locals meant them harm. A ship carrying crusaders across the Mediterranean Sea sank suddenly, killing about four hundred people. And all the travelers encountered other problems as well, such as winter weather, a lack of food, and exhaustion.

Given the hardships, quite a few crusaders changed their minds about the journey not long after starting out. Their decisions were roundly mocked by some chroniclers, who lost no time explaining the penalties these people would face. "Fearing the future," one wrote, "many of our people . . . returned home like cowards. For this, they were held worthless by God as well as men, and they became utterly disgraced." Disgrace, cowardice, and damnation were strong punishments indeed. Yet the flow of warriors heading back to western Europe continued.

Quoted in Michael Foss, *People of the First Crusade*. New York: Arcade, 1997, p. 73.

on the Muslims, but there were too many Western soldiers and commanders to absorb them all. Furthermore, Alexius was unwilling to place his own troops under the leadership of the rough and reckless Western leaders. Alexius therefore suggested that the Westerners do the bulk of the fighting on their own, while the Byzantines provided support and reinforcements. The Frankish leaders agreed.

In April 1097 most of the crusader armies began moving eastward. To reach Jerusalem, a distance of more than 700 miles (1,100km), they first needed to make their way through present-day Turkey, a Seljuk stronghold. In May they attacked the city of Nicaea, the capital of the region. The Muslim ruler of the city, Kilij Arslan, knew the Franks were on their way, but he believed that these soldiers would be no more skilled than the peasants led by Peter the Hermit. By the time he realized his mistake, it was too late. With help from Byzantine soldiers, the crusaders besieged the city; that is, they surrounded it, preventing people from getting out and supplies from getting in. The siege was successful, and Nicaea soon surrendered. Jerusalem, it seemed, would be easily within the crusaders' grasp.

The Siege of Antioch

Next, the troops defeated Kilij Arslan's army at a place called Dorylaeum. The crusaders exulted. Muslims throughout the region, on the other hand, were deeply distressed. "When the news was received," wrote a Muslim historian soon afterward, "the anxiety of the people became acute and their fear and alarm increased."[16] Muslims noted that the crusader army had a relatively open path south toward the city of Antioch, not far north of Jerusalem. They hastened to send soldiers and weapons to Antioch in hopes of stopping the Christian advance.

After a difficult journey involving poor roads, hunger, and a steady series of quarrels, the Frankish leaders reached Antioch late in 1097. Following yet another argument over the proper course of action, they besieged the city as they had done at Nicaea. Antioch did not fall quickly, however. Compared to Nicaea, it had stronger defenses, more supplies, and a larger army. Nor were the crusaders able to close off access to the city completely. Still, they were willing to wait.

Weeks and months drew on, however, without any sign of surrender. Indeed, the Christians suffered some significant problems as time passed. Food remained an issue, especially with the onset of winter, and some soldiers died of hunger. Others were killed in skirmishes with the Muslim troops in Antioch, and more died when Muslim reinforcements arrived from other parts of the Middle East. Discouraged, the surviving crusaders wondered whether to continue. "The poor began to leave," wrote a chronicler, "and also many of the rich who feared poverty."[17]

Then, in June, the Franks got unexpected help. One of Antioch's guards secretly made contact with a Western knight named Bohemond. This guard had a grudge against Antioch's Muslim governor. He promised to help Bohemond and his troops invade the city, and he kept his word. One night, he set ladders against the city walls to allow the Christians access. Once some of the crusaders were inside, they opened a gate to let others pour in. After a fierce and bloody battle, the Christians massacred as many Muslims as they could find. At last, they controlled Antioch.

The surviving Muslim soldiers quickly assembled outside the city walls. Then, with help from reinforcements, they began a siege of their own. Badly outnumbered, the Christians stood little chance of breaking through the Muslim siege. And with little food in Antioch, they began to starve. When everything seemed at its bleakest, though, a miracle occurred—a miracle in the eyes of the Franks, at least. Two crusaders had visions in which they learned that the Holy Lance—a spear supposedly used to pierce Jesus' side as he hung dying on the cross—was buried within the city. "Whoever shall bear this lance in battle," the visionaries were told, "shall never be overcome by an enemy."[18]

The crusaders did indeed find a spear beneath the ground. Muslim chroniclers charged afterward that the whole thing was an elaborate hoax designed to lift the spirits of the Christians. There had been no visions, they argued, and the spear

the crusaders unearthed had been placed there a few days before. Whatever the true story, the discovery gave the Christians renewed confidence. On June 28 the Franks charged out of Antioch. Surprised, the Muslim armies fought back, but they could not coordinate their efforts. Before long they were retreating across the countryside. The Christians had saved themselves—and strengthened their hold on the city.

Jerusalem

The crusaders spent the summer and fall in Antioch. As usual, they spent most of their time arguing. Some thought they should restore Antioch to Alexius, as they had promised. Others wanted to offer it to Pope Urban instead. Two of the leaders wanted the city for themselves. The Franks also quarreled about what to do next. Some advocated going on to Jerusalem as soon as possible; others counseled patience. Making matters worse, disease ravaged the troops all summer, and the fall brought further food shortages.

In the end, the group split. In January 1099 some of the crusaders set off for Jerusalem, leaving others behind. Those who moved on were soon beset by further

An Antioch guardsman helped Bohemond and his troops invade the city. A battle ensued, which is depicted in this painting, and the Christians gained control of Antioch. The Muslims fought back, but despite their efforts, the Christians strengthened their hold on the city.

This illuminated manuscript page shows the conquest of Jerusalem in 1099. The Christians recaptured Jerusalem, ending the First Crusade.

quarrels, and various factions headed off in different directions. Disease, hunger, battles, desertion, and the perpetual arguments had sharply diminished the number and effectiveness of the Franks by this time, yet the Christian force moved steadily southward. They took the city of Latakieh on the east coast of the Mediterranean, then the city of Tripoli farther south, and continued to advance.

In June 1099 the first group of crusaders reached Jerusalem. Anticipating a siege, the Muslim ruler of Jerusalem, Iftikhar al-Daula, stocked up on food and forced all the city's Christians to leave. He also poisoned the wells outside the city, eliminating the crusaders' supply of fresh water, and he sent out an urgent call for reinforcements from other Muslim groups. In the meantime the crusaders set up their camps outside the city walls and, as a knight proudly put it, "began to besiege the city in a marvelous manner."[19]

But when the Muslims did not surrender quickly, the Franks decided not to wait as they had at Antioch. Instead, they began to build siege towers—tall wooden structures that could be dragged to city walls and then used like ladders. In mid-July, the towers complete, they staged an assault on the city. At first, the Muslim defenders fought off the Christians, but when a few crusaders successfully made it across the wall, the momentum shifted. Before long, Iftikhar surrendered. Jerusalem, the holiest city in Christendom, had been recaptured.

The Christians reacted to their victory by going on a rampage. They killed every inhabitant of the city they could find, soldier and civilian, Muslim and Jew; the Jews, they charged, had given help to the Muslim soldiers. The crusaders' brutality was horrifying. Nonetheless, a French priest recorded the details with approval. "Men rode in blood up to their knees and bridle reins," he wrote. "It was a just and splendid judgment of God that this place should be filled with the blood of the unbelievers. . . . The city was filled with corpses and blood."[20]

The First Crusade was over, but the battle for the Middle East had only begun.

Chapter Three

Holy Wars, Holy Warriors

Following their victory at Jerusalem, the Franks divided their conquests into four small kingdoms or states, each governed by one of the nobles who had gone on the crusade. Many of the soldiers then headed for home. They were weary of travel, weary of the endless bickering, and—at least in some cases—weary of war. Others, however, chose not to return to Europe right away. These men stayed in the Middle East to set up the new kingdoms, to extend their boundaries, and to defend them against attack.

Problems

It seemed that the crusaders were now in a powerful position. They had successfully taken much of the Middle East. They had demonstrated their military skill, their eagerness to fight, and their intent to destroy their enemies. However, Christian control of Jerusalem and the other three outposts was actually quite shaky. The Christian victory in the First Crusade had been possible in part because so many troops had been involved. Now that most of those soldiers had gone home, the new crusader territories were not well protected. As one chronicler wrote, "There were not enough people to defend [Jerusalem] from the Saracens [Muslims], if only they dared to attack us."[21]

Moreover, the Muslims were in a potentially much better position than it appeared at first glance. The Franks had taken Jerusalem in part because different Muslim groups could not act as one. Some Muslims actually supported the crusaders in their battle against the Seljuks, who they perceived to be a more dangerous enemy than the crusaders—and a more immediate one as well. If the various Muslim groups had banded together to fight the Franks, it is doubtful that the crusaders could have reached Jerusalem, let alone taken it. The Muslims had not been unified, however, and the Christians took advantage of that fact.

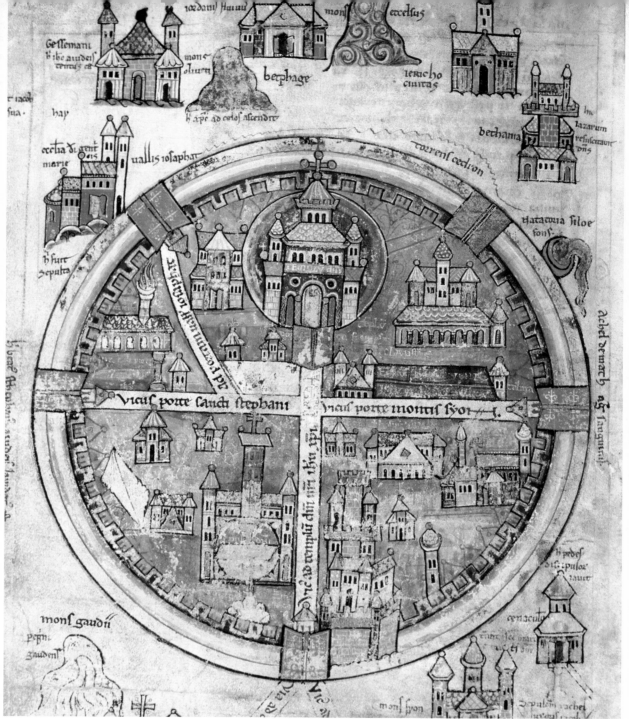

The crusaders had successfully taken Jerusalem from the Muslims, but problems were beginning to arise. The Muslims were starting to become more unified, which posed a potential threat to the Christians.

There was no guarantee, however, that the Muslim world would stay divided. By and large, the Muslims in the region lamented the loss of Jerusalem. Many blamed the divisions in Islam for the defeat, too. As one writer sorrowfully put it, "Discord between the Muslim princes enabled the Franks to overrun the land."[22] The brutal massacre of Jerusalem's Muslims also served to bring the various factions together. The slaughter angered and horrified the Islamic world and sparked cries for revenge against the Christian invaders. For now, however, the Muslims were not yet unified enough to launch any serious attack on the new crusader states.

Life in the East

Both sides soon adapted to the realities of a shared Middle East. Surrounded as they were by Muslims, Jews, and Eastern Christians, the Franks slowly adopted a few Eastern cultural practices. They changed what they ate and how they dressed. Some married local women or began learning local languages. A new generation grew up that had never visited Europe and knew relatively little about it. "We who were Occidentals [that is, Westerners]," concluded one Christian chronicler just twenty years after the end of the First Crusade, "now have been made Orientals,"[23] or Asians.

At the same time, many Muslims accommodated themselves to the realities of Christian rule. Several Islamic leaders traded with the Christian principalities and signed peace treaties with the crusaders. Some ordinary Muslims were relieved to discover that the Franks did not usually interfere with the practice of Islam in their new possessions. A few developed reasonably close friendships and personal connections with the Franks, though these connections did not always translate to understanding of the Christians' ways.

Other Muslims, however, found it harder to accept things as they were. They bitterly complained about fellow Muslims who did not resist the invaders, especially those who seemed happier under Christian rule than they had been when ruled by Muslims. "Their hearts have been seduced," wrote one commentator. "The Muslim community bewails the injustice of a landlord [that is, a ruler] of its own faith, and applauds the conduct of its opponent and enemy, the Frankish landlord."[24] For these Muslims, the First Crusade had been a terrible disaster. It had weakened the Muslim people and had put the Franks into an intolerable position of power.

Zengi Takes Edessa

The fragile peace between the Christians and the Muslims did not last. In the 1120s a Muslim leader known as Zengi came to prominence in the northern Middle East. Zengi was smart, forceful, and ambitious, and his first goal was to gain power within the Muslim world. Zengi's initial targets were two cities in present-day Syria, Aleppo and Damascus. Both were held by other Muslim groups, and Zengi wanted them both.

Aleppo fell easily, but Damascus withstood repeated assaults from Zengi's

Military Orders

In the wake of the First Crusade, the Christian victors created two special organizations known jointly as the Military Orders. One was called the Knights Templar. It was a military force pledged to do the work of God in the world, which meant ensuring that Christian pilgrims would be able to travel freely throughout the Middle East. It also meant attacking Muslims and others who seemed to be enemies of the Christians. As historian Zachary Karabell describes it in his book *Peace Be upon You*, the Templars "represented the fusion of the soldier and the priest."

The other order was known as the Knights Hospitaller. Though the Knights Hospitaller did have some military responsibilities, it was more focused on medical care, as its name suggests. These two organizations survived for many years, appearing frequently in narratives of the Crusades written by participants and chroniclers. Over time they gradually became more and more independent of church control. At the same time, they built up remarkable stores of wealth. Today these groups, especially the Templars, have become what Karabell calls "crusader icons"—the source of the romantic, dashing image of a crusader common in modern society.

Zachary Karabell, *Peace Be upon You: Fourteen Centuries of Muslim, Christian, and Jewish Coexistence.* New York: Alfred A. Knopf, 2007, p. 104.

The Knights Templar were part of the organization known as the Military Orders.

troops. The people of Damascus were dedicated fighters, and the city had been built with sturdy walls to keep invaders out. Moreover, the rulers of the city had established a military alliance with—of all people—the Christians in Jerusalem. It was an extremely odd pairing from a religious perspective, of course, but it made military sense for the Christians and the leaders of Damascus alike. With the help of the Franks, the Damascans were able to keep Zengi and his army away.

Frustrated with his inability to conquer Damascus, Zengi turned his attentions elsewhere. In 1144 he decided to attack Edessa, the smallest and weakest of the four crusader states. The timing was right. The king of Edessa, Joscelin II, could count on little help from outside his territory. Nearby Christian leaders were either feuding with Joscelin or were distracted with other concerns. Better yet, Joscelin had just led his armies into battle against another Muslim group, leaving the kingdom unguarded. It was a foolish decision, and one that would cost Joscelin dearly. "Towers, walls, and earthworks are of little value to a city," pointed out a Christian chronicler, William of Tyre, "unless there are defenders to man them."[25]

In December Zengi and his men besieged Edessa. They dug a trench beneath a city wall, propped it up with wooden sticks, and then set the sticks on fire. That caused the wall to collapse, and in the ensuing panic and confusion the Muslims entered the city. They killed some of the Christian inhabitants, took others prisoner, and—for reasons that are not entirely clear today—left most of the rest alone. After close to fifty years, one of the crusader states had fallen into Muslim hands.

The Second Crusade

The news that Edessa had fallen reached Rome in 1145. Western Christians were outraged. Eager to strike back against the Muslim enemy, Pope Eugene III quickly began making plans for a second Crusade. This time, the crusaders would reclaim Edessa and strengthen the Christian hold on the other crusader states. Two kings volunteered to lead the crusade. One was Louis VII of France, the other a German ruler known as Conrad III.

The two leaders gathered soldiers and supplies and discussed plans. They agreed to travel separately and to join forces when they reached Byzantium. The Germans left first and arrived in Byzantium in the fall of 1147. Manuel I Comnenus, the Byzantine emperor, was not at all pleased to see the twenty thousand or so German troops marching into his city. Like Alexius before him, Manuel distrusted the Western Christians and worried that they might attack Byzantium instead of moving on. Accordingly, Manuel urged Conrad not to linger, but to head immediately toward the Middle East.

Conrad was always quite eager for action, and he very much liked this idea. He divided his soldiers into two groups

King Louis VII of France and King Conrad III of Germany volunteered to lead the Second Crusade. King Louis VII is pictured here receiving the pilgrim's staff from Pope Eugene III before leaving for the Second Crusade.

and sent them toward Edessa by different routes, reasoning that the French would soon catch up and make the crusader army extremely hard to beat. Neither of the German groups got very far, however. One group ran low on supplies as it made its way across the Muslim-held sections of Turkey. In October 1147 members of this group were attacked by Seljuk Turks, and hundreds of crusaders died. The other group was routed as well in a battle early in 1148. Only a small fraction of the crusaders made it past the Seljuks. Conrad had failed.

The French Arrive

The French armies, led by Louis VII, were not far behind Conrad. They too moved quickly through Byzantium, especially after Manuel refused to provide the crusaders with fresh soldiers. Late in 1147 the French marched into Turkey. There they joined forces with Conrad and his few remaining troops. Again, though, the Seljuk Turks blocked their path.

Louis decided to travel the remaining distance by sea. He went to a nearby port and boarded a ship to make the short journey across the eastern Mediterranean. Louis took only a small number of crusaders with him, though, and those who remained in Turkey were soon attacked and overcome by the Seljuk Turks. Most of the soldiers who survived this battle returned home, recognizing that they could not easily break through

Prester John

During the crusades, Christian leaders began hearing tales of a powerful Christian king, long separated from the rest of Christianity, who ruled extensive lands somewhere beyond the borders of Europe. The name of this king was Prester John. Not much was known about Prester John; his kingdom was located in central Asia, some said, but others believed that it was in Africa, and still others asserted that Prester John's lands lay even farther to the east. Nor did anyone know exactly how Prester John had lost contact with the rest of Christianity.

Still, the rumors of Prester John intrigued the Franks. It was possible that this mighty king might come to the aid of the crusaders, if he could only be located. The prospect of a strong army attacking the Muslims from another direction was very appealing. Accordingly, envoys began trying to find Prester John. Their search was doomed to failure, however, and years later it became evident that no such kingdom existed. Most likely, the crusaders had heard reports of small Christian enclaves in Ethiopia or central Asia and had allowed themselves to exaggerate the importance of these communities. In any case, Prester John never did make an appearance.

The siege of Damascus (pictured) was a failure. The crusaders' failed attempt to claim Damascus only served to antagonize its citizens and to increase Muslim unity.

the Seljuk defenses. Only a few crusaders continued on to reach the safety of Jerusalem. Even counting Louis and those who accompanied him over the seas, the crusaders were now just a small fraction of their former numbers.

Once in Jerusalem, these remaining crusaders conferred with the leaders of Jerusalem. The goal of the crusade, of course, had been the recapture of Edessa, but now the Christian knights abruptly changed their plans. Instead of moving toward Edessa, they decided to attack Jerusalem's recent ally, Damascus. Zengi had died two years earlier, and the crusaders believed that his kingdom was al-

ready dwindling in power. Moreover, the Franks had seen the military strength of Damascus up close. As a result, the Christians now believed that Damascus was the greatest threat to the three surviving crusader states. The reclaiming of Edessa could wait.

Along with forces from Jerusalem, the crusaders headed toward Damascus and besieged the city. The leaders of Damascus got help from other Muslim groups nearby—most notably, from Nur ad-Din, Zengi's son and the heir to his kingdom. The display of Muslim unity was an ominous sign for the crusaders, especially given the recent hostilities between Zengi and the leaders of Damascus. In the face of the combined Muslim armies, the crusaders could not hold their positions. They began bickering among themselves. Before long they gave up and went back to Jerusalem, pursued all the way by Muslim fighters.

The Second Crusade was at an end. It had hurt the crusaders considerably. Thousands of soldiers were dead, and Edessa was still under Muslim control. The French, the Germans, and the people of Jerusalem all blamed each other for the failed siege of Damascus. Perhaps worst of all, the crusaders had antagonized Damascus, only recently an ally of Jerusalem, and had drawn the Muslims of the Middle East closer toward military cooperation. In all, the Second Crusade was a disaster.

Two More Leaders

The leaders of the Second Crusade had made another error, too. They had believed that the Muslims of Damascus represented the greatest threat to Christianity in the Middle East, but they were wrong. The greatest threat was Zengi's son, Nur ad-Din.

Like Zengi himself, Nur ad-Din was a powerful leader who worked hard to expand his territory and influence. Beginning in 1147, he had formed alliances with several Muslim groups east of the crusader states, alliances that he either dominated or hoped to dominate before long. Later, he staged two raids against the Christian kingdom of Antioch, killing one of its leaders and taking some of its territory. "All the Muslims far and wide were in ecstatic joy"[26] when they heard the news of Nur ad-Din's success, claimed a Muslim chronicler of the time.

Then, in 1154, Nur ad-Din dissolved his temporary alliance with Damascus and captured it, thereby accomplishing what his father could not. Over the next fifteen years, Nur ad-Din extended his power further still, eventually taking Egypt and several other territories. Little by little, he was establishing himself as the leader of all the region's Muslims. At the same time, he staged several more attacks on Antioch and the crusader state of Tripoli, though he left Jerusalem alone. Few doubted that he or his successors would eventually try to eliminate the crusader states altogether.

Nur ad-Din died in 1174 and was succeeded by his most powerful assistant, Saladin. Saladin was well respected among Muslims of the time; in the eyes of some, he was very nearly beyond human. A Muslim observer of the time wrote a description of Saladin that began by listing an enormous number of positive attributes and ended by noting that this list included only "a few examples of his soul's lofty and noble qualities." The list omitted most of Saladin's characteristics, the writer continued, "in order not to extend this book unduly and bore the reader."[27]

Like Nur ad-Din, Saladin was eager to continue uniting Muslims into a single cohesive group—under his own leadership, of course. Part of Saladin's goal was to obtain political power, but he had a deeply religious motive as well. Bringing the Islamic world together, Saladin said, was not simply his own desire; it was Allah's. "We have come to unite the word of Islam," he explained, "and restore things by removing differences."[28]

Jihad

For Saladin, uniting Islam meant ignoring or removing the differences between the various Muslim groups. It also meant eliminating the crusader states—and, if possible, the Byzantine Empire as well. He envisioned the Christian cities of the region falling one by one to the power of the Muslims, until, as Saladin put it, the Islamic faith had "wiped the world clean, turning the churches into mosques."[29]

Saladin did not act against the Christians for several years, however. He waited until he had been seriously provoked. In 1185 a Jerusalem knight named Reynald of Chatillon led an unsuccessful attack against the two holiest cities of Islam, Mecca and Medina. This attack infuriated Saladin. A year later, Reynald captured a caravan of Muslim traders and took them prisoner. According to some sources, one of Saladin's sisters was among the captives. Already angry over the attack on Mecca, Saladin asked Reynald to release her. Reynald, however, refused.

Now Saladin was furious. He declared a holy war, also called jihad, against the Christians of the Middle East. He summoned men from all over the Middle East to carry out their duties as Muslims and take up arms against the unbelieving Christians. In July 1187 an army of Muslims assembled near Jerusalem. A Christian chronicler noted that the men were "as numerous as the sands of the seashore."[30]

Still, the king of Jerusalem, Guy of Lusignan, was not dismayed. He had the help of soldiers from Antioch and Tripoli as well as the men of Jerusalem itself. His knights had strong horses and heavy armor. Most important of all, they carried the True Cross—the cross on which Jesus had supposedly died. To the crusaders, the cross was a signal that God was with them. They believed they could not lose as long as they had it.

A Great Victory

July was hot in the Middle East, and water was scarce. Saladin cleverly drew the heavily armored crusaders out of Jerusalem in pursuit of the Muslim troops. That led the Franks away from water supplies and trapped them in the desert at a place called the Horns of Hattin. Saladin's troops now set fires nearby, filling the air with thick smoke, and shot arrows through the fire. "Throughout the night," lamented a Frankish observer, "the hungry and thirsty [crusaders] were harassed . . . by arrows and by the fire's heat and flames."[31]

In the morning, the Muslims staged a direct attack. The Christians were soundly defeated, and the True Cross was taken from them. Many knights were killed in the fighting. Others fled. Still others, including Guy and Reynald, were captured by Muslim forces. Guy was imprisoned, but Reynald met a different fate. According to one Christian's account, Reynald responded rudely when Saladin offered him something to drink. Saladin then became enraged. "Pig!" he shouted. "You are my prisoner, yet you answer me so arrogantly?"[32] Drawing his sword, he killed Reynald on the spot—and followed that

up by sentencing another few hundred Christian knights to be executed as well.

Jerusalem, Tripoli, and Antioch were still in Christian hands. Still, after the defeat at the Horns of Hattin, it was obvious that the crusaders could not counter Saladin's power. In the coming weeks, Saladin's army conquered one Christian fortress after another. Only a few were able to keep the attackers away. In September the Muslim army besieged Jerusalem. The Christians of the city recognized that they could not win. After negotiating for some time with Saladin and his assistants, they surrendered in exchange for Saladin's promise to spare their lives.

For Saladin, that was a reasonable trade. He had no desire for bloodshed in this case. Even though Islam had holier cities than Jerusalem, Jerusalem was nevertheless a sacred place for Muslims. As Saladin told the Christians, "I believe that the city is God's abode, as you believe. It would be much against my will to lay siege to the house of God or put it to the assault."[33] Indeed, Saladin kept his word. He held many Christians for ransom and sold others as slaves, but there was no repeat of the massacre of eighty-eight years earlier, when Jerusalem had most recently changed hands.

In one sustained campaign, Saladin had all but destroyed Christian power in the Middle East. From Saladin's perspective,

Saladin's power grew as he defeated the Christians time and again. His army reclaimed Jerusalem and destroyed much of the Christian power in the Middle East.

The Persecution of the Jews

The Second Crusade, like many others, was marked by persecution of the Jews on the part of Christian soldiers. In part, this was sparked by a perception that the Jews were giving less than their fair share in support of the Crusades. There was plenty of hostility toward Jews in Europe under the best of circumstances, and the violence of the Crusades helped bring that out. This contemporary report indicates the level of brutality faced by some of Europe's Jewish population:

They rose in a spirit of cruelty against the Jewish people . . . and slaughtered them without mercy, especially in the Kingdom of Lorraine [in France], asserting it to be the beginning of their expedition and their duty against the enemies of the Christian faith. This slaughter of Jews was done first by citizens of Cologne [in Germany]. These suddenly fell upon a small band of Jews and severely wounded and killed many; they destroyed the houses and synagogues of the Jews and divided among themselves a very large amount of money. When the Jews saw this cruelty, about two hundred in the silence of the night began flight by boat. . . . The pilgrims and crusaders discovered them, and after taking away all their possessions, inflicted on them similar slaughter, leaving not even one alive.

Quoted in August C. Krey, *The First Crusade: The Accounts of Eye-Witnesses and Participants*. Gloucester, MA: Peter Smith, 1921, p. 55.

the news was all good. He was the acknowledged leader of Muslims throughout the region. As he had hoped, Muslims had banded together to carry out the will of Allah. Only a few outposts remained under Christian control. The Muslim holy war had been a magnificent success.

By declaring holy war against the Christians, however, Saladin had raised the stakes in the conflict. The mutual respect that had been part of Middle Eastern life, even after the First Crusade, was slipping away. Alliances between Christians on the one hand and Muslims on the other had essentially disappeared. Victory in battle was no longer just about gaining territory or holding prisoners for ransom; it was proof of Allah's greatness, proof of the power of God.

The Crusades had been a religious battle from the beginning. Now that was truer than ever. As a result, the positions of both sides were becoming ever more entrenched.

Chapter Four

Richard and Saladin

If the taking of Edessa had distressed the Christians of western Europe, the conquest of Jerusalem was even more alarming. After almost a century, the Christians had lost control of the Holy City. To many in the West, this was intolerable. At one time, compromise might have been possible, but tensions between Christians and Muslims had risen sharply during and after the Second Crusade. Even if Saladin were to guarantee the right of Christians to live in Jerusalem and make pilgrimages to the Holy Land, the Europeans seemed unlikely to be satisfied with anything less than full control of the city.

To the Franks, moreover, maintaining ownership of Jerusalem was no longer just a matter of religion; it was a matter of honor. Stories of the bravery and the might of the original crusaders continued to circulate throughout western Europe. Knights and nobles had grown up knowing that the men of the First Cru-sade had sacrificed their lives and endured terrible hardships to win Jerusalem for Christians and their descendants. Now those descendants had lost the prize the original crusaders had struggled so hard to obtain. By giving up control of Jerusalem, the Christians of 1187 had failed their ancestors.

The Third Crusade

Given the hostilities of the previous hundred years, there was only one possible response by the Christians in Europe to the loss of Jerusalem. That, of course, was to fight. Pope Gregory VIII lost no time in organizing a Third Crusade. Although the nobles and princes of Europe were, as usual, arguing among themselves, Gregory implored them to settle their grievances and unite against their common Muslim enemy. He used powerful rhetoric to convince his people of the danger. "Those savage barbarians," he noted of the Muslims, "thirsted after

Christian blood and used all their force to profane the holy places and banish the worship of God from the land."[34]

Gregory's appeal had a strong effect. He convinced three important European leaders to take on the responsibility of leading the crusade. One of these men was Philip Augustus, the king of France. Philip hoped to sweep the Muslims out of Jerusalem, but he had two other motivations as well for doing Gregory's bidding. For one, Philip wanted treasure; he hoped to return from the Middle East with silver and gold taken from the Muslim enemy. For another, he wanted to increase his power and prestige. Leading a crusade seemed a good way to accomplish these two goals.

The second king was a German named Friedrich I Barbarossa; *Barbarossa* was a nickname that meant "Red-Beard." Friedrich was perhaps the single most respected man in all of Europe at the time. He had taken part in the Second Crusade; he was the nephew of Conrad, the German king whose army had been destroyed while attempting to cross present-day Turkey. Though he was nearing the age of seventy, Friedrich was eager to travel to the Holy Land once more—this time, he hoped, with a better result.

Henry and Richard

The third king was Henry II of England. However, Henry did not get along well with Philip of France. At the time, England controlled large sections of what is now France, so the two kings argued frequently about territory. Moreover, they were the two most powerful leaders in the northwestern part of Europe. In the violently competitive culture of the medieval era, that was all that was necessary to make them enemies.

Philip soon saw an opportunity to eliminate his rival. Henry's son Richard—known today as Richard the Lionhearted—wanted desperately to be the next king, but he suspected that Henry preferred John, one of Richard's brothers. In early 1189 Philip offered to help Richard overthrow his father. With the help of Philip's army, Richard forced Henry to name Richard his successor. "God grant that I may not die until I have had my revenge on you,"[35] Henry is said to have told Richard; but Henry's health was poor, and he died soon afterward, giving Richard control of the kingdom. The new king started making plans to take his father's place at the head of the proposed crusade.

Philip, Richard, and Friedrich were among the best leaders that Europe had to offer. They made up a powerful team for the upcoming assault on the Holy Land. On the other hand, the Muslim forces were impressive, too, and their leader, Saladin, seemed a match for any of the three western European kings. The clash between these men and their armies promised to be monumental.

Pope Gregory VIII appealed to three European kings, Philip Augustus of France, Friedrich I Barbarossa of Germany, and Henry II of England, to lead the Third Crusade. However, Philip and Henry II (pictured here) did not get along, and Philip quickly helped Henry's son Richard overthrow his father.

Saladin and the Byzantines

The Crusades were marked by frequent changes of alliances between the warring parties—including, of course, alliances between Christians and Muslims. One of the most intriguing of these was a possible connection between Saladin's Muslims and the Christian leaders of Byzantium. During the Third Crusade, Saladin was especially alarmed by the army of Friedrich Barbarossa. Expecting that Friedrich would pass through Byzantium, Saladin made overtures to the Byzantines about forming a possible coalition against the Germans. He hoped that the Byzantines might hinder Friedrich, even if they could not stop him altogether, and he likewise hoped that the Byzantines might support him if the German army reached the Holy Land.

The Byzantines were tempted. They were not enthusiastic about yet another Western army tramping through their territory, and they also recognized that an alliance with the Muslims would reduce the possibility that Saladin would attack Byzantium. In fact, the Byzantines did make a few attempts to slow down Friedrich. In the end, however, mistrustful as they were of Friedrich, the Byzantines decided they trusted Saladin even less. The proposed alliance never materialized.

Friedrich and the Germans

Early in 1189, Friedrich Barbarossa sent a letter to Saladin explaining his intent to attack and warning the Muslims that they faced a powerful army. "You, God willing," he wrote, "shall learn by experience the might of our victorious eagles, and be made acquainted with our troops of many nations."[36] In May Friedrich began to lead his twenty thousand or so soldiers toward the Middle East. They were the first of the three groups to depart.

Friedrich's forces were indeed strong. One historian has called the German soldiers "the best-trained and best-equipped army yet known to the Crusades."[37] By the spring of 1190, the army had pushed its way to a spot only about 100 miles (160km) from Jerusalem. No Muslim force had yet been able to do more than harass it, and Saladin was not sure he could keep his new possessions in the face of this mighty army—and its powerful leader. For Friedrich was quite proud of his own physical abilities and had noted in his letter to Saladin that he had the strength and vigor of a much younger man. "You shall assuredly be taught that our own right hand, which you suppose to be enfeebled by old age, can still wield the sword,"[38] he boasted.

In truth, however, Friedrich was no longer in top-notch condition, and the journey had taken its toll. In June, while

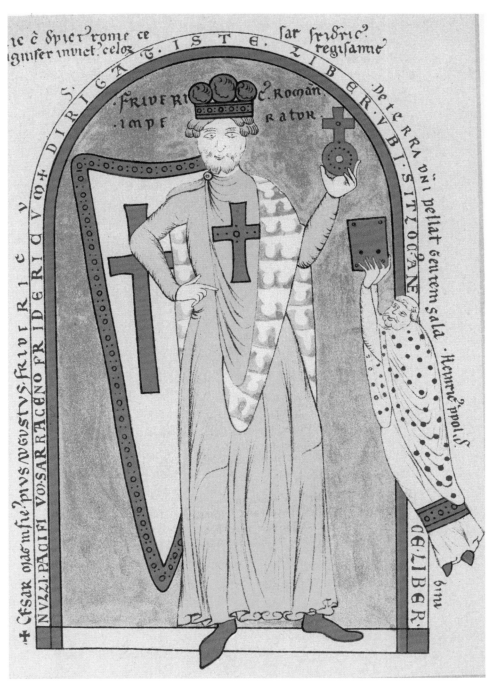

Friedrich Barbarossa led a powerful army in an attempt to reach the Holy Land. However, before the army could reach Jerusalem, Friedrich died unexpectedly and many of his soldiers returned to Germany.

leading his army across a river, Friedrich unexpectedly fell into the water and drowned. Christians and Muslims alike were shocked to hear the news. It had seemed to people on both sides that Friedrich was larger than life, if not immortal. A Muslim chronicler wrote with surprise that Friedrich had "drowned at a place where the water was not even up to his waist."[39]

That was the end of Friedrich—and the end of the mighty German army, too. Shaken by their leader's death, and unable to find a new commander to replace him, the soldiers lost their confidence and their sense of purpose. Many returned home. Only a few reached the Holy Land. The Muslim reaction to Friedrich's death, in contrast, was one of relief. As one historian writes, "All Islam saw the hand of God in this miraculous demise."[40] It seemed that Allah had come to the aid of his people by destroying Friedrich's army.

Another Attempt

The English and the French both planned to reach the Holy Land by crossing the Mediterranean Sea. They stopped in Sicily, an island southwest of Italy, where they began to bicker over Philip's sister, Alice. Earlier, Richard had expressed interest in marrying Alice. Now, partly at the urging of his mother, a powerful queen known as Eleanor of Aquitaine, Richard had decided instead to marry a princess from Spain. Philip felt betrayed by his former ally. The incident caused a rift between the two men.

In March 1191 the French army left Sicily. Within a month these crusaders reached Tyre, one of the few remaining Christian possessions in the Middle East. They were enthusiastically welcomed by the Christians of the region. At the time, many of the Frankish knights who remained in the Middle East were besieging Acre, a port city that had until recently been a Christian possession. Philip and his men quickly joined the siege. For the first time in several years, the Christians of the Middle East had reason for optimism.

That optimism was boosted by the knowledge that Richard was on the way. But while this expectation heartened the Christians, it dismayed the Muslims. Richard was already well known as a fighter and a leader. One Muslim ruler knew of him as "a man of great courage and spirit [who] showed a burning passion for war."[41] With Friedrich Barbarossa dead, Richard seemed to be the greatest remaining threat to Saladin's authority.

In fact, Richard did not actually reach the Holy Land until mid-June. Always eager for battle, he had made an unscheduled stop at the Mediterranean island of Cyprus to dethrone a ruler closely connected to the Byzantine emperor. Still, when they finally arrived, Richard's forces made an immediate difference. The Middle Eastern Christians who were besieging Acre had already been joined by Philip's men as well as by the remnants of Friedrich's army, now commanded by Leopold of Austria. The English forces tipped the balance.

Saladin was outside the city walls, unable to help the people in Acre, but Muslim swimmers occasionally braved the Mediterranean currents to carry messages back and forth between Saladin and the soldiers in the city. Aware that the Muslims were losing, Saladin implored the soldiers to fight harder. As one Muslim chronicler put it, however, "the army did not support him, for the enemy infantry stood like an unbreakable wall."[42] Instead, over Saladin's objections, the defenders of Acre surrendered.

The English, the French, and the remnants of Friedrich's army captured Acre, a city that had been a Christian possession but had recently been taken over by the Muslims.

Opposing Armies

The Christian soldiers of Richard's army and the Muslim troops who made up Saladin's fighting force were bitter enemies. But as historian Zachary Karabell points out in his book Peace Be upon You, *hostility was not the only part of the story:*

Camped near each other, the knights and commoners of each side fraternized during the long periods of inactivity. According to some accounts, the combatants would even stop fighting in the middle of a battle if they perceived that neither side had the upper hand. Arms would be laid down; there would be conversation and storytelling; one side would extend an invitation to dinner. At other times, contests were held to see who had more prowess in the arts of war, and then all would celebrate the winners.

As with the proposed marriage of Richard's sister to Saladin's brother, these connections between the troops indicated that the Third Crusade was not entirely based on religious hatred. The soldiers, at least on occasion, were able to see the humanity of the men on the other side and enjoyed their company as well.

Zachary Karabell, *Peace Be upon You: Fourteen Centuries of Muslim, Christian, and Jewish Coexistence.* New York: Alfred A. Knopf, 2007, p. 131.

Surrender and Dissension

As winners of the battle, the Christians dictated the terms of the surrender. They insisted that the Muslims return the True Cross, which had been taken from the Franks at the Horns of Hattin. They also demanded silver and gold in exchange for allowing the Muslims safe passage out of Acre. The Christians put a very short time limit on gathering the funds and bringing the cross to Acre, however. When Saladin and other Muslim leaders could not come up with the full sum right away, Richard gleefully took revenge: He ordered the execution of about three thousand of the best Muslim sol-

diers. Then he and Philip divided the money the Muslims had managed to find and let most of the other Muslims go.

Though they still did not have the True Cross, the Christians were exultant. During the dark days of the Second Crusade, the Christians had feared that God had abandoned them. Now it seemed that God was working on their behalf after all. "The Christians . . . entered the city without opposition," wrote a chronicler, "glorifying God, and giving Him thanks, because He had magnified His mercy to them."[43] For now, at least, the Christians were unified and triumphant.

Those good feelings did not last long, though. The fault was entirely Richard's. As one historian puts it, "The King of England was doing what he did best, apart from fighting, which was to make unnecessary enemies."[44] Soon after the surrender, Richard saw an Austrian banner above a tower. It had been put there by order of Leopold of Austria, the new commander of Friedrich's remaining troops. Richard, however, was infuriated. Unwilling to share the victory with anyone else, Richard demanded that the flag be pulled down. Leopold immediately left for home, taking his troops with him.

Before long, Richard and Philip were quarreling again, too. The victory at Acre had given Philip the treasure he wanted, and he informed Richard of his desire to go home. Richard responded by accusing the French king of cowardice. "If he leaves undone the work for which he came hither," Richard complained, "he will bring shame and everlasting contempt upon himself and upon France."[45] Even so, the two men eventually worked out a deal. Philip would leave most of his troops with Richard, who would be responsible for paying them. Thoroughly disgusted with each other, Richard and Philip parted ways, and Philip returned to France.

Richard was now the undisputed leader of the Christian troops, and he still had his eyes set on Jerusalem. In August 1191 he left Acre and moved south with his army. Saladin's forces moved alongside the Christians, harassing them at every opportunity. The weather was hot and the going was slow, yet the crusaders kept moving toward their goal—and the Muslims stayed right with them along the entire route.

Problems

The two armies were well matched, and so were their commanders. Both Richard and Saladin were intelligent, bold, and well versed in military strategies. At the same time, both faced some significant problems. Not all of Richard's men were happy with his leadership. Nor was Richard sure his army was powerful enough to defeat the Muslim armies. That remained true even after the crusaders defeated the Muslim forces in a battle in mid-September.

Saladin had troubles, too. A few Muslim nobles worried that Saladin was losing his touch as a commander. Several of his assistants began challenging him on military matters. Some of his soldiers blamed him for not having stopped the massacre that followed the siege of Acre. Arguing broke out among various Muslim factions; as one Muslim of the time wrote, "the Kurds will not obey the Turks and the Turks will not obey the Kurds."[46] As time passed, Saladin became less sure that he could defeat an opponent as brave, as committed—and as bloodthirsty—as Richard.

The First and Second Crusades had been marked by one dramatic and gory battle after another. Both sides had accepted nearly every military challenge that came their way. They had attacked, besieged, harassed, and marauded, even when doing so seemed to make very little military sense. Now, with the siege of

Richard and Saladin made an attempt at ending the fight over Jerusalem without war but eventually returned to battle when the two sides could not reach an agreement.

Acre behind them, Richard and Saladin began doubting themselves. The armies continued south toward Jerusalem, but cautiously. The daring of the earlier battles had vanished.

Indeed, diplomacy became more important than ever before. At one point Richard and Saladin seriously discussed a proposal to end the fighting and to settle the problem of Jerusalem once and for all. Richard suggested that his sister Joan marry Saladin's brother, creating a joint Muslim-Christian union that would be in charge of Jerusalem. The idea made some sense. In effect, Jerusalem would become a neutral territory. Moreover, the marriage would join the two warring families, making them allies and defusing the hostility between them.

In the end, Richard's proposal went nowhere. Joan was bitterly against marrying a Muslim and convinced many powerful nobles to support her against Richard. Nor is it likely that Saladin would have permitted his brother to marry a Christian. Furthermore, the two sides probably did not trust one another enough to share control of Jerusalem. Saladin and Richard soon gave up talks and returned to battle. Nonetheless, the episode demonstrates that even at this point in the conflict, the advancement of religion was not the only motivation for the two sides. That Richard and Saladin could consider a solution such as this, at the height of what they both considered a holy war, speaks to the complexity of the Crusades.

Fighting—or Not

In November 1191 the crusaders took a small fort on the outskirts of Jerusalem. They were certainly near enough by now to stage an attack on the city itself, but Richard decided against an assault. Fearing that his army lacked the strength to oust the Muslims from Jerusalem, he ordered a retreat, much to the disgust of many of his soldiers. Saladin, in turn, considered attacking the retreating crusaders. But he did not attempt this either. Earlier, such caution would have been unthinkable. Now, well aware of their own weaknesses, both commanders had become much less willing to take risks.

In May 1192 Richard tried again. He and his men once again came within a few miles of Jerusalem. Had he attacked, he might have taken the city. The Muslims

Richard, pictured on his way to Jerusalem, twice avoided a direct attack on the city in November 1191 and May 1192. Instead, he helped defeat Saladin's army at Jaffa.

were quarreling among themselves, and it is clear today that Saladin held little hope that his army could hold off the crusaders. However, Richard did not make the attempt. In part, he was distracted by troubles at home; he had recently learned that his brother John was trying to take over his kingdom. Rather than stage an assault, Richard retreated to Acre. There he began making plans to leave the Holy Land altogether.

Before he could leave, though, Richard received word that Saladin had attacked a Christian stronghold called Jaffa. Richard hurried to help, but he found that Saladin's armies were already in the city. Yet Richard did not hesitate. Now, at last, he regained the courage and audacity that had made him famous. Supported by only a handful of men, he led a charge against the Muslims and pushed Saladin's army out of Jaffa. Muslims and Christians alike agreed that Richard was the main reason for the victory. "The king was a giant in the battle and everywhere on the field,"[47] reported a Christian commentator.

Truce

Still, Richard did not follow up on his victory with another push toward Jerusalem. Besides being anxious about what was happening in Britain, he was by now physically and emotionally exhausted. He had lost the support of his French troops, too, and he was, as usual, arguing with other Christian leaders. In any case, Richard was not sorry about the results he had achieved. He had put Jaffa, Acre, and other regions back un-der Christian control, and he had helped shore up the other Christian possessions in the Holy Land. In Richard's eyes, he had done all he could, and he was ready to leave for England.

With neither side interested in fighting any longer, Saladin and Richard quickly hammered out a peace treaty. The crusaders kept most of the territories they had conquered. Both sides agreed that for three years neither would attack the other. Saladin also promised to let Christian pilgrims enter Jerusalem unmolested. Richard then set sail for Europe, though he made sure to issue a threat to Saladin before he left: Someday soon, he promised, he would come back with an even stronger army. Saladin gallantly replied that he would prefer to lose his empire to Richard than to any other king.

In an ideal world, peace might have prevailed once more between Islam and Christianity in the Middle East. True, the Christians did not control Jerusalem, and the Muslims had not pushed the Christians out of the region altogether. Still, those did not need to be insurmountable obstacles; the two sides had lived together in relative harmony before, and they certainly could do so again.

In reality, however, circumstances had changed. Both sides continued to believe they were fighting a holy war. These beliefs made a true, long-term compromise unacceptable to Christian and Muslim alike. The conflict would continue. Its next expression, however, would take a form that no one on either side could have anticipated.

Chapter Five

The Fourth Crusade

For a few brief years following the Third Crusade, the Middle East remained relatively peaceful. That was not because the two sides were getting along, though, or because either Christians or Muslims were relaxing their uncompromising hostility toward each other. Rather, the peacefulness was entirely practical. Neither the Muslims nor the Christians were in a position to launch any sort of serious attack.

That was perhaps especially true of the Muslims. Even Saladin had been unable to maintain their unity during the later stages of the Third Crusade. Then, a few months after signing the truce with Richard, Saladin died. His death left a leadership vacuum among the Muslims and increased the level of bickering among the remaining groups. The Muslim forces needed to work together if they were ever going to retake the entire Holy Land. Cooperation, however, did not seem to be on any Muslim leader's agenda at that moment.

Nor did the Christians start a new crusade right away. The most likely candidate to lead another assault on Jerusalem was Richard, but he had other, more immediate concerns. On his way back to England in 1192, he was taken prisoner by an alliance of Austrians and Germans. When he finally returned home more than a year later, he was distracted by political issues and could not travel to the Middle East. In 1196 Friedrich Barbarossa's son Henry led an army toward Jerusalem, but Henry died along the way, and his soldiers gave up the attempt and went back home instead.

Still, passions were too inflamed to lie dormant for long. In 1198 a new pope came to power. Known as Innocent III, he was intelligent and well spoken, and he was an ardent enemy of Islam and its power in the Middle East. Like the crusaders before him, Innocent lamented the loss of parts of the Holy Land to the "unbelievers" and longed to see it returned to Christian control. Later that year, Innocent announced a new crusade to regain Jerusalem and rid the Middle East of Muslim rule.

Innocent's Appeal

Innocent appealed to western European sensibilities very much as earlier popes had done. He asserted that God was on the crusaders' side and that it was a moral and spiritual obligation to fight for Christian supremacy. He told European nobles and knights that Saladin had taken not only Christian lands but Christian honor as well, and that it was up to them to reclaim it. "Receive the shield of faith and the helmet of salvation," he preached. "Trust not in numbers [of soldiers], but rather in the power of God. . . . Come to the aid of Him through whom you exist, live and have being."[48]

The Third Crusade had ended just six years earlier. Going on a crusade, therefore, was not an abstraction as it had been for the men who ventured to the Holy Land during the first three Crusades. European nobles knew very well what crusading implied: a long and difficult journey, years apart from family and friends, the risk of death and disease, and much more. As a result, some nobles refused to go. But others were swayed by Innocent's arguments. Like those who responded to earlier calls, they hoped to win God's favor and earthly respect by conquering Jerusalem, and they hoped to return home with gold and silver taken from the Muslims as prizes of the war.

The nobles decided to travel to the Holy Land by sea, as Philip and Richard had done a few years earlier. That route was several hundred miles shorter than the land route through eastern Europe, and if the winds were favorable, travelers could move much more quickly by ship than by marching overland. The sea route also seemed safer. Not only would sea travel allow the crusaders to avoid the Muslim-controlled areas of Turkey, but the crusaders would also stay away from the Byzantine Empire. In the previous few decades, the quarrels between Byzantium and the Western Christians had intensified. Richard the Lionhearted's quick trip to depose a Byzantine ruler on Cyprus during the Third Crusade had only made things worse. It seemed foolish for the crusaders to try to travel through Byzantium this time.

There was an issue, however. The nobles who were joining the Fourth Crusade mostly came from northern Europe, especially northern France and Germany. They did not have ready access to the Mediterranean Sea. Nor did they have long seafaring traditions. They were without the ships—and the know-how—to transport such a large army to the Holy Land. Accordingly, they turned to Italy for help.

The Duke of Venice

The cities of the Italian peninsula were the richest and most refined that the West had to offer. Towns such as Venice and Genoa were important trading centers and strong seafaring powers. The merchants of these towns carried goods and people between western Europe, Byzantium, and the Holy Land. They had close

Enrico Dandolo, the doge, or duke, of Venice, and the crusaders reached an agreement in Venice. Dandolo agreed to give the crusaders warships in exchange for eighty-five thousand marks (currency) and a promise that they would travel to Egypt first.

ties to some of the Muslim-held regions of the Middle East as well. It made sense for the crusaders to hire the Italians to organize a convoy across the Mediterranean for them.

In 1202 six representatives of the crusaders traveled to Venice. They met with Enrico Dandolo, the doge, or duke, of Venice. Dandolo was about ninety at the time and blind, but his mind was sharp and his wealth extensive, and he was sympathetic to the crusaders' cause. The crusaders begged Dandolo to "take pity on the land overseas . . . and graciously do your best to supply us with a fleet of warships and transports."[49] After much discussion and negotiating, Dandolo agreed to do as the crusaders asked.

Dandolo did make one significant change to the plan, though. He insisted that the crusaders not sail directly to the Holy Land, as Richard and Philip had done several years before. Instead, he stipulated that the nobles travel first to Egypt. After conquering the Muslim leaders of that country, Dandolo said, the crusaders could then move north and east toward Jerusalem. This plan made some sense from a military perspective. Controlling Egypt would increase Christian influence in the Middle East and make a recapture of Jerusalem by the Muslims much less likely. Moreover, it seemed wise to approach the Holy Land from an unexpected direction. Dandolo's main reason for heading to Egypt, however, was commercial. Egypt was a wealthy trading center, and Dandolo longed to control the trade in and around the region.

The crusaders told Dandolo that 33,500 men would join the army. Thus, hundreds of ships would be needed to transport soldiers, horses, food, and other supplies. That would cost an enormous amount of money, especially because many of these ships would have to be built specifically for the journey. Dandolo calculated the cost at eighty-five thousand marks (currency), about twice the annual income of a powerful European king. The contract called for the crusaders to pay the full sum no matter how many soldiers actually appeared.

The representatives did not worry about how they might pay. They formally accepted the terms in an emotional ceremony. "The Doge and all the [crusaders] burst into tears of pity and compassion," wrote Geoffrey de Villehardouin, one of the six representatives, "and cried with one voice, and lifted up their hands, saying 'We consent, we consent!'"[50] Then the representatives hurried back north to tell the nobles and the pope of the agreement.

The Siege of Zara

Over the next few months, the crusaders gathered troops and raised money—much of it from extra taxes on Jews. In 1202 contingents of men began arriving in Venice, ready for the trip ahead. It soon became apparent, though, that Christian leaders had miscalculated. There were far too many ships for the number of soldiers present. As de Villehardouin put it, the fleet "could easily have accommodated three times as many men as were in the whole army."[51] Some knights had opted to make their

Dandolo's crusaders stormed the city of Zara in 1202. Dandolo had suggested that the crusaders conquer the city in order to confiscate the wealth needed to pay him for his warships.

own way to the Middle East. The main issue, however, was that the original estimate of 33,500 soldiers was overly optimistic. The crusade's leaders could not find anywhere near that many soldiers.

This presented a major problem. The Venetians had spent freely to build ships in anticipation of the crusade. They had put aside some of their own commercial activities to do so as well. Thus, Dandolo was unwilling to reduce the price he charged the crusaders. On the other hand, the crusaders had planned to charge each soldier for his own passage in order to obtain the marks they owed the duke. Without the expected number of soldiers, they had no way to make up the shortfall.

Dandolo had an idea, however. Venice had been feuding for some time with the leaders of a wealthy European city called Zara, across the Adriatic Sea from Venice. For years, Dandolo had wanted to control the city and its wealth. He suggested that the crusaders sail to Zara and conquer the city. By plundering Zara, they could get the money to pay the Venetians. Once their debt to the duke was settled, the crusaders could then head toward Egypt. Most of the crusaders agreed, and they soon sailed for Zara.

Pope Innocent, however, was deeply distressed when he heard the news. Not only did this side trip strike him as a distraction from the crusaders' real goal, but Zara was a Christian kingdom—and a kingdom affiliated with Rome rather than with Byzantium, at that. Innocent did what he could to stop the crusaders. "I forbid you to attack this city," he told the troops, "for the people in it are Christians."[52] A few crusaders did heed the pope's words. Agreeing that they had not signed up for the crusade in order to attack Christians, they remained in Venice or went back home.

Most of the crusaders, however, were willing to fight. The reality was that the travelers owed Venice much more money than they could pay. If the expedition was to reach the Holy Land, it had to find the funding somewhere; and Innocent, for all his strong talk, could not offer an alternative source of money. These crusaders besieged Zara, conquered it, and confiscated much of its wealth. Even so, the proceeds were not nearly enough to pay everything that the crusaders owed Dandolo. Furthermore, the conquest had led to dissension among the crusaders—and dissatisfaction on the part of the pope.

Prince Alexius

At this point, Dandolo and the crusaders received an intriguing message from Prince Alexius of Byzantium. Alexius was the nephew of Emperor Alexius III, who ruled the Byzantine Empire at this time. The two men were enemies, however; the emperor had deposed the prince's father several years earlier. Prince Alexius had escaped to western Europe, but he wanted to be returned to the throne. He asked the crusaders for help overthrowing his uncle. In exchange, he promised them what they needed. "Since [Alexius] is aware that you have spent all your money and now have nothing," one of his envoys wrote,

In exchange for being put on the throne, Prince Alexius of Byzantium offered Dandolo and the crusaders two hundred thousand marks and provisions for their armies.

"he will give you 200,000 silver marks, and provisions for every man in your army."[53]

A few of the crusaders agreed that Alexius's offer was worth taking. The plan, one argued, "afforded the best means by which the land overseas [that is, Jerusalem] might be recovered."[54] Most of the assembled crusaders, however, were reluctant. To put Alexius on the throne, they might be forced to fight their fellow Christians. The attack on Zara had been difficult enough to justify. The crusaders were on a holy quest, and to make two separate attacks on different Christian groups seemed unacceptable to many of the travelers. Besides, Byzantium was much more powerful than Zara. An attack on Byzantium might leave the crusaders too weak to defeat their real target, the Muslims.

An emotional discussion now erupted within the crusaders' ranks. It was clear that the majority of the crusaders wanted to reject Alexius's offer, even if that meant walking to the Middle East. "Everyone was shouting that we should make haste for Acre [that is, go directly to the Holy Land]," wrote one participant, "and there were not more than ten who spoke in favor of [Byzantium]."[55] Those who argued for accepting Alexius's proposal, however, included some of the most powerful crusaders. In the end, these men prevailed, though a number of the crusaders withdrew from the expedition.

On to Byzantium

The remaining crusaders spent the winter of 1202–1203 in Zara. In May 1203 they sailed for Byzantium, along with some of their Venetian allies. "So fine a sight had never been seen before," de Villehardouin noted approvingly. "As far as the eye could reach there was nothing to be seen but sails outspread on all that vast array of ships."[56] In the next few weeks, the travelers moved slowly eastward. Along the way, they captured several cities and territories belonging to the Byzantines. By mid-June, the crusaders had arrived at Byzantium itself.

The combined forces of the crusaders, their Venetian allies, and the Byzantine soldiers affiliated with Prince Alexius now besieged the city. For a while the emperor's defenses held, but the Venetians set a fire that destroyed part of Byzantium, and the Byzantine army abandoned an attack that might have pushed the crusaders away from the city walls altogether. Before long, the people of Byzantium lost their patience with the emperor and rose up against him, forcing him to leave the city. Prince Alexius marched into the city in triumph and claimed the throne as Emperor Alexius IV.

All that remained was for the new emperor to pay the crusaders and the Venetians the money he had promised. But Alexius had difficulty coming up with the funds. His uncle had taken much of the royal treasury with him when he left Byzantium—half a ton of gold by some accounts—and there was not enough remaining to settle Alexius's debts. To make up the difference, Alexius raised taxes on the Byzantines, a move that proved extremely unpopular. He also ordered that many religious statues be melted down and converted to silver and gold. This decision was unpopular as well. Nor did either measure make up the entire amount that Alexius owed.

Over the next few months, tensions worsened. The Byzantines resented Alexius's rule; they even more deeply resented the presence of the crusaders and the Venetians. The crusaders, in turn, grew steadily more impatient as they waited for Alexius to fulfill his promises. Alexius begged the crusaders to grant him a six-month extension, which they did reluctantly. Fighting between the crusaders and the Byzantines routinely broke out, however, in and around the city.

"This War Is Lawful and Just"

The situation changed abruptly, though, in January 1204, when Alexius was himself deposed—and murdered—by a Byzantine leader known as Mourzuphles. Mourzuphles was an opponent of the crusaders, and he immediately informed them that he did not consider himself bound by Alexius's promise. Instead, he launched an attack against the Westerners and pushed them out of Byzantium altogether. Some of the crusaders interpreted this defeat as a sign that God disapproved of their attack on Byzantium and the Christians who lived there. They were ready to return home.

The clergymen who helped lead the expedition sharply disagreed, however. Mourzuphles, they pointed out, had no right to kill Alexius. Moreover, they added, the Byzantines were the religious enemies of the western Europeans, their shared Christian beliefs notwithstanding. After all, the clergy pointed out, the Byzantines had refused for generations to submit themselves to the rule of Rome. "Wherefore we tell you," they concluded, "that this war is lawful and just."[57] In other words, it was not simply acceptable, but required, for the crusaders to try to overthrow Mourzuphles.

Reassured that God was indeed on their side, the crusaders fell to this task with great enthusiasm. Their first assault against Mourzuphles, however, met with no success; the Byzantines drove the crusaders back with little difficulty. Mourzuphles was delighted. "Never did you have so good an emperor!" he boasted to his advisers. "Have I not done well? We need fear [the crusaders] no longer. I will have them all hanged and dishonoured."[58]

The crusaders quickly regrouped, however. In April 1204 they staged another attack on Byzantium. This time, after some brutal fighting, they managed to make their way into the city. The crusaders now launched into a series of violent acts against the local population, acts every bit as vicious as those the original crusaders had carried out against the Muslims and Jews of Jerusalem. Blood ran freely; cries of terror filled the streets. "On every hand the [Byzantines] were cut down," wrote de Villehardouin. "So great was the number of killed and wounded no man could count them."[59]

The Sack of Byzantium

The crusaders also set to work ransacking the city. Now that Byzantium was in the crusaders' hands, the western Europeans

Weapons

Christian and Muslim armies during the Crusades typically used the same kinds of weapons. Most soldiers relied heavily on swords, especially when the two sides had come quite close together. Both Christian and Muslim knights were well trained in the art of swordsmanship, and those soldiers who could handle a sword with particular skill and flair were accorded tremendous respect. Many soldiers also used lances, long spears that were particularly effective when used by riders on horseback.

Bows and arrows were in common use as well. Both Muslims and Christians used plenty of archers. Their main job was to stand behind the front lines and pelt the opposition with sharp-tipped arrows. The shooters used complex bows that could launch arrows a long way. They usually could not win battles by themselves, but they could pick off invaders as they came over a city wall or through a narrow mountain pass, and they could harass the swordsmen of the other side.

The most effective weapons of the time, though, were larger and more imposing. During the siege of Byzantium, the crusaders created siege towers—tall structures that could be rolled or dragged to the wall of a city—allowing soldiers to damage the wall or climb over it. The Christians also built enormous catapults and used them to fling heavy objects at the city's walls, gradually breaking them to pieces. As for the

Byzantines, they used catapults, too, but they also dropped boulders and boiling oil onto the heads of crusaders trying to climb the walls of the city. By modern standards, the weapons of the Crusades were rough and often unwieldy. Still, they did the job they were meant to do.

During the time of the Crusades, weapons known as catapults were used to fling heavy objects at city walls.

The crusaders attacked Byzantium in April 1204, terrorizing the city in a bloody siege.

carried off whatever they could—and destroyed much of the rest. From the crusaders' perspective, they had every right to do as they pleased. Because the Byzantines had failed to pay what they owed, the destruction was no less than the Byzantines deserved. Besides, the crusaders believed, the sack of Byzantium was God's will. "So those who denied us small things," noted one chronicler with satisfaction, "have relinquished everything to us by divine judgment."[60]

To the rampaging crusaders, nothing was sacred; no place was off-limits. Much of the looting was for the purpose of gathering treasure, but much was simply destruction for its own sake. The crusaders pulled statues off the walls of churches. They smashed windows, knocked down walls, and leveled entire buildings. The city's great library was essentially demolished, and with it volume after volume of priceless and irreplaceable texts. For three days and nights the sacking continued, with gangs of crusaders prowling the city—often drunk on the Byzantines' wine—and damaging everything they could.

The Spoils of War

I n theory, the treasures the crusaders took from Byzantium were to be shared equally. In reality, though, that did not happen. The crusaders pooled more than enough of their booty to pay off the debt they owed the Venetians. The majority of the loot, however, was not shared; instead, it wound up in private hands. "Many there were, both great and small," wrote Geoffrey de Villehardouin, "who kept back part of the spoils, and it was never known."

De Villehardouin was quick to point out that the leaders of the Franks punished those who were caught concealing treasure. "And as to theft, and those who were convicted thereof, you must know that stern justice was meted out to such as were found guilty, and not a few were hung." Yet as de Villehardouin recognized, few were caught. The reality was that much of the wealth of the Byzantines was smuggled back to Europe to enrich the pockets of minor European nobles and merchants. Even if the crusaders had continued to Egypt or the Holy Land, the riches pillaged from the Byzantines would have contributed very little to the spread of Christianity or the defeat of the Muslims.

Geoffrey de Villehardouin, *Memoirs*, trans. Frank T. Marzials. London: J.M. Dent, 1908, p. 66.

The remaining Byzantines were appalled. One Byzantine despairingly described the crusaders as "war-maddened swordsmen, breathing murder . . . pillaging the holy places, trampling on divine things, [and] running riot over holy things."[61] Trying to interfere was dangerous; many Byzantines were killed for speaking up against the destruction, let alone attempting to stop it. The inhabitants of Byzantium could only look on helplessly as the crusaders commandeered their horses, their homes, their food, and even their clothing, and took their city apart, bit by bit. "There never was a greater crime against humanity than the fourth crusade,"[62] writes historian Steven Runciman; and while he may have been exaggerating for effect, his basic point remains valid.

The sack of Byzantium marked the effective end of the Fourth Crusade. The crusaders chose a count named Baldwin to rule the much-diminished city. Then, abandoning their goal of freeing Jerusalem, they returned to their homes. Most were pleased by the blows they had struck for Christ and for Rome. Dandolo was among them. Though events had not worked out quite as the Venetian leader had planned, he was delighted with his share of the Byzantine treasury. Of those most involved in the expedition, the most disappointed was probably Pope Innocent. He had opposed the notion of a detour to Byzantium from the beginning; now that the detour had become the only journey, he was doubly enraged. He had no power, however, to discipline the nobles who had gone against his wishes.

In the end, the Fourth Crusade had had nothing whatever to do with the religious fervor that had marked the previous three. The Muslims were not even involved, and fighting took place exclusively between Christians and Christians. For years, the Crusades had been partly a struggle of religion and partly a struggle of economics and politics. At times, the religious disagreements had stood out. Now the economic and political reasons for the Crusades were coming to the fore. The Fourth Crusade had settled nothing; indeed, it had made the situation in and around the Middle East more complicated than ever before.

Chapter Six

The End of an Era

The Fourth Crusade had brought no changes to the Middle East itself. From the Christian perspective, the situation in the Holy Land was still a grave concern. Jerusalem, after all, remained firmly in Muslim control, and the Franks still held only small sections of the Middle East. Thus, it was only a matter of time before the next crusade got under way.

But in truth, Westerners were beginning to change the way they thought about crusading. It was becoming increasingly apparent that no Western force could succeed in dislodging the Muslims from the Middle East for long. The victories of the First Crusade had been real, but fleeting. The Second Crusade had been a disaster, and Richard's mighty army had never launched an attack on Jerusalem during the Third Crusade. As Westerners saw more and more clearly the futility of their quest, the excitement of knights and churchmen for further adventuring diminished. The story of the crusades during the 1200s reflects this gradual loss of interest.

The Fifth Crusade

The Fifth Crusade was the most popular of all the campaigns that followed the Fourth Crusade. It was announced, once again, by Pope Innocent. Innocent was still smarting over the results of the Fourth Crusade. The leaders of this expedition had not followed Innocent's instructions at all, of course, and the pope was eager to send out another group of knights and nobles that would do as he asked. In 1213, therefore, he issued a call for a new crusade to reclaim Jerusalem.

Innocent offered the now-familiar promise that the sins of those who took part would be forgiven, and he extended this promise to wealthy men who gave money to the expedition as well. He also called for peace within western Europe. In his eyes, the fighting that had racked the various kingdoms of the region distracted

Pope Innocent III issued the call for the Fifth Crusade with the hope that the Christians would reclaim Jerusalem.

Christians from their more important goal and needed to stop. Finally, he demanded that Christians stop trading with Muslims, and he promised a harsh penalty indeed to those who did not obey. "We excommunicate . . . those false and impious Christians," he wrote, "who, against Christ himself and the Christian people, carry arms, iron, and wood for ships to the Saracens,"[63] or Muslims.

The men of the Fifth Crusade decided to attack the Muslims on two different fronts. One was near Jerusalem. A group of crusaders set sail for the city of Acre and tried to march toward Jerusalem. The Muslims, once again, were disorganized and could not push the crusaders back. Indeed, some of the Muslims living in Jerusalem evacuated the city, afraid that the Franks would capture it and repeat the massacre of the First Crusade. The Christians formed an alliance with a group of Seljuk Turks, ironically enough. Even so, they never managed to get close enough to Jerusalem to capture the city.

Egypt

The other focus of the crusaders was the northern coast of Egypt, where the men of the Fourth Crusade had intended to go. To the leaders of this crusade, an as-

Crusades Elsewhere

The best-known and best-remembered crusades were fought in the Middle East. But popes and European political leaders were also eager to reclaim Spain, much of which had been taken over by Muslim armies. Even while some knights and nobles contended with the Muslims in Jerusalem and Egypt, others traveled to Spain in order to drive the Muslims back across the Mediterranean Sea—or to exterminate or convert them instead. Some of these crusades were actually quite successful, viewed from the perspective of the Christians, though it was not until 1492 that the Muslims were forced to leave Spain for good.

As time went on, the term *crusade* became less and less meaningful. In 1208 Innocent III started a crusade against a group of Christians in southern France. These people were heretics—that is, they did not accept the official word of the pope on several spiritual matters—and the purpose of the crusade was to restore them to the fold. A few years later, Friedrich II of Germany became the target of another crusade, less for religious reasons than because of his growing power and authority. And when the Mongols began sweeping into eastern Europe in the 1230s, the pope called for a crusade against them as well. By the end of the 1200s, a crusade meant almost any war with any kind of religious or ethnic overtones.

sault on Egypt still made good sense, and in June 1218 they besieged a coastal city called Damietta. For months, though, they were unable to dislodge the Muslims who were Damietta's rulers. In the meantime, disease ravaged both sides, killing and weakening many of the soldiers. By 1219 the leaders of both the Christians and the Muslims were dead.

The new Muslim ruler, a man known as al-Kamil, now made a remarkable offer. Desperate to maintain his hold on Damietta, he proposed a trade with the Christians. If the crusaders would promise to stop attacking Damietta, he would arrange to cede another city to them. That city, as it happened, was Jerusalem. Astonishingly, though, the new Christian leader, a man named Pelagius of Albano, rejected the offer. Pelagius apparently believed that he could capture both Damietta and Jerusalem. Not all the other crusaders agreed with him, however. Appalled by Pelagius's decision, several of these men left for home.

In November 1219 Damietta finally fell to the crusaders—the first conquest of importance during the six years since Innocent had made his appeal for a new crusade. The crusaders wasted their advantage, however, by arguing among themselves for a year and a half before moving on to attack the even larger prize of Cairo. The delay allowed al-Kamil to gain important allies from among the nearby Muslim groups. On the way to Cairo, the Christians encountered bad weather, unexpected flooding, and other obstacles; but mostly, they encountered a fresh and angry fighting force.

The Muslims pushed the crusaders back and forced them to surrender, reclaiming Damietta in the process. Al-Kamil then signed a peace treaty in which he allowed the Franks to go home, if they agreed not to attack Egypt again for at least another eight years. The only concession he made to the crusaders was a promise to return to them a piece of the True Cross. The joke was on the crusaders, however, as this relic did not actually belong to al-Kamil or any of his allies. In the end, then, the men of the Fifth Crusade came away from their adventure with absolutely nothing to show for their troubles.

Friedrich Succeeds

The next attempt to recapture Jerusalem came just a few years later, and it was much more successful than any since the First Crusade. This crusade, generally known as the Sixth Crusade, was led by Friedrich II, a powerful German king who had a vested interest in Jerusalem. In 1225 Friedrich had married Yolanda, the daughter of John of Brienne. Christians considered John to be the king of Jerusalem; at least, he would have held kingly powers had the Christians controlled the city. If Friedrich could help restore his father-in-law to the throne, he would add immeasurably to his own influence and authority.

In 1228 Friedrich set sail for Acre. To this point, popes had supported—or indeed called for—all the crusades, but Friedrich did not have this support. Indeed, Pope Gregory IX forbade Friedrich to go. Gregory's objections, however, had nothing to do with religion. Instead, they

were purely political. Friedrich had been feuding with the papacy for quite some time, and his influence within Europe approached that of the pope. Gregory worried that a successful crusade would make Friedrich the most powerful man in Europe. Gregory even excommunicated Friedrich in hopes of forestalling the expedition.

Friedrich was not intimidated. He arrived in Acre to a warm welcome and began planning an attack on Jerusalem. Many knights native to the Middle Eastern principalities eagerly signed up to help. When news of Friedrich's excommunication reached the Holy Land, however, some of his support began to dwindle. Excommunication was serious business. Besides, the pope had many allies in and around Acre, and they did not want to seem too hospitable to Gregory's bitterest enemy.

The withdrawal of support from those loyal to the pope forced Friedrich to change his plans. With fewer troops than he had anticipated, Friedrich marched his troops up and down the coast near Acre, pretending that his army was larger than it actually was. His hope was to intimidate the Muslims in the area and make them willing to negotiate with him. His bluff was successful. Upon seeing Friedrich's show of force, the Muslim ruler of Jerusalem offered to cede some

Pope Gregory IX excommunicated Friedrich II in the hope that he would not participate in the Sixth Crusade and attempt to recapture Jerusalem.

control of the city to the Christians in exchange for a promise not to attack. The two sides eventually hammered out an unusually generous agreement in which Friedrich allowed the Muslims to maintain their hold on certain sections of the town and also safeguarded the rights of Muslims to visit the city: "The Saracens [Muslims] of that part of the country," he wrote, "since they hold the temple in great veneration, may come there as they choose in the character of pilgrims."[64]

There was no mistaking who was now in charge of the city, however. For the first time since Saladin had taken Jerusalem in 1187, the city was back in Christian hands. Friedrich lost no time informing his European allies and foes about his achievement, though he piously attributed his success to divine intervention. "Jesus Christ, the Son of God," he wrote, "beholding from on high our devoted endurance and patient devotion to His cause, in His merciful compassion of us, at length brought it about that the sultan of Babylon [the Muslim leader] restored to us the holy city, the place where the feet of Christ trod."[65]

King Louis

But Friedrich soon returned to Europe, and Christian control of the city did not last long. In 1244 a Muslim group from Turkey besieged the city and conquered it. This attack was based much less on religious differences than on military gain; the Turks were traveling toward Egypt and simply saw an opportunity for conquest. Nonetheless, western Europeans interpreted the attack as yet another Muslim assault on Christianity. One commentator noted that the assault had been the work of a "barbarous and perverse race."[66] Even so, no Western leaders immediately called for another crusade. A year passed before the French king, Louis IX, announced a crusade to reclaim the city yet again.

Louis was a wealthy and powerful king, and he put together an expedition that one historian has called "impressive . . . well-organized, [and] well-financed."[67] In 1249, after careful planning, Louis and his men arrived in Egypt, their initial target. Like the people of the Fifth Crusade some years before, Louis now attacked Damietta, which he took with little difficulty. Louis then marched on toward Cairo and other Egyptian cities. Once again, this proved to be a mistake. Louis's army was defeated by a Muslim group known as the Mamluks, allies of the Turks who had conquered Jerusalem. Instead of attempting to return to the safety of Damietta, Louis compounded his error by trying to besiege another Egyptian city with the remnants of his army. The crusaders suffered miserably from disease and hunger, and they were soon routed by the Muslim defenders of the city.

When Louis finally did head for Damietta, moreover, he was taken prisoner by Muslim soldiers. Louis's assistants had to pay an enormous sum of money to the soldiers to obtain his release. His army in tatters, his treasury nearly empty, and his crusade a failure, Louis now traveled to Acre to add his remaining troops to the defense of the crusader states. He returned to Europe in

King Louis IX arrives in Egypt on horseback. Louis claimed Damietta but was defeated when he tried to take other Egyptian cities.

1254, thus marking the end of what most historians call the Seventh Crusade.

Louis Returns

By this time, the enthusiasm for crusades among the western Europeans had cooled noticeably. Although Christians in the West continued to wish for Christian rule in the Middle East, it was increasingly clear that the ownership of Jerusalem had very little real impact on anyone's life outside the Holy Land. Nor had the crusades of the 1200s, even Friedrich II's Sixth Crusade, reduced the supposed menace posed by the

Christian armies defend the city of Acre from the Mamluks. In 1291 the Muslims captured Acre, leaving the Christians without any possessions in the Middle East.

Muslims. On the contrary, the crusades seemed to bring mainly death, hardship, and failure. "After the defeat of . . . Louis in 1250," writes one historian, "preachers of a crusade were publicly insulted"[68]—a far cry from the overwhelming acceptance and excitement earlier recruiters had encountered.

Indeed, times had changed. In 1265 a powerful Mamluk sultan named Baybars started taking Middle Eastern Christian strongholds one by one. In earlier days, the conquest of even one of these Christian possessions would have sparked a furious response by thousands upon thousands of Western soldiers. In the 1260s, however, few Westerners seemed to care. The only significant response, in fact, came from King Louis, who led yet another army to Egypt in 1270. Louis reached the Muslim-held city of Tunis in present-day Tunisia, where he and his assistants managed to negotiate for somewhat better treatment for the Christians who lived in the city. It was a worthwhile achievement, even if it did nothing to help the crusader states to the east; but it was the expedition's only accomplishment. Late in 1270, Louis became ill and died.

Conceivably, Louis could have done more if he had lived. Realistically, though, he had little chance of reconquering Jerusalem, or even of doing much to maintain the survival of the crusader kingdoms against Baybars. Louis had too few troops and too little support from other kings and nobles—and, for that matter, from the pope. Nor is it clear that Louis truly expected major accomplishments. According to one historian, this Eighth Crusade was fought mainly for personal reasons: It stemmed from Louis's "attempt to purge his feelings of guilt"[69] about his failure some years before.

Whatever the truth, the Eighth Crusade ended with Louis's death, and with it ended the era of the crusades. Over the next few years the remaining crusader

The Fall of Acre

The capture of Acre in 1291 is described here by a Christian chronicler, eager to make the point that the defenders of the city might have held off the Muslim army if they had worked together.

There were at that time in the Sultan's army six hundred thousand armed, divided into three companies; so one hundred thousand continually besieged the city, and when they were weary another hundred thousand took their place . . . [another] two hundred thousand stood before the gates of the city ready for battle, and the duty of the remaining two hundred thousand was to supply them with everything that they needed. The gates [of the city] were never closed, nor was there an hour of the day without some hard fight being fought. . . . But the numbers of the Saracens [Muslims] grew so fast that after one hundred thousand of them had been slain two hundred thousand came back. Yet, even against all this host [the Muslim army], they [the Christians] would not have lost the city had they but helped one another faithfully; but when they were fighting [outside] the city, one party would run away and leave the other to be slain, while within the city one party would not defend the castle or palace belonging to the other, but purposely let the other party's castles, palaces, and strong places be stormed and taken by the enemy, and each one knew and believed his own castle and place to be so strong that he cared not for any other's castle or strong place.

Quoted in James Brundage, *The Crusades: A Documentary Survey.* Milwaukee: Marquette University Press, 1962, p. 270.

states in the Middle East grew gradually weaker, and the Mamluks around them grew more and more bold. Yet the Christians of the West still launched only half-hearted attempts to help, and sometimes not even those. "With want of enthusiasm, want of new recruits, want, indeed, of stout purpose," writes historian Morris Bishop, "the remaining Christian principalities gradually crumbled."[70] In 1289 Tripoli fell to the Mamluks. In 1291 the Muslims besieged the last Christian possession, Acre, and captured it as well. For the first time since the First Crusade two centuries earlier, there were no Christian outposts in the Middle East.

Impact

The Crusades had come to an end. On one level, the two centuries of attacks had accomplished very little. The valor of the early crusaders, the courage of Saladin's Muslims, the brutality and violence of the battles, the religious fervor that had marked the campaigns—all had changed nothing. True, thanks to the men of the Fourth Crusade, Rome now held the upper hand in its spiritual and political struggle with Byzantium, and the Mamluks, rather than the Seljuks or the Kurds, were now in the ascendant among the Muslims. But two hundred years of bitter struggle between the Christians and the Muslims had not altered the basic balance of power between those two groups. Before the Crusades, Muslims had held the entire Holy Land. With the fall of Acre, that was true once again.

Partly because of this, some historians have concluded that the Crusades had little effect on world history. The warfare, they point out, was concentrated in a relatively small area running from Byzantium along the Mediterranean coast to Egypt. Daily life for the people of the area did not change significantly when one side or the other claimed or reclaimed territory. Nor was the Middle East engulfed in constant fighting through the two hundred years of the Crusades. Indeed, peace reigned through most of this period. Historian Zachary Karabell writes that the real story of the Crusades lies in the "decades of live-and-let-live that separated the brief but exciting episodes of armies mustering, sieges laid, and battles fought."[71]

On another level, however, the Crusades had an enormous impact on the world. The expeditions helped raise European awareness of the world beyond its borders. At a time when few western Europeans traveled even to nearby countries, the crusaders were visiting Byzantium, Egypt, and the Middle East, and they were making their way by land across Hungary, Italy, and Greece. The tales they told about these distant lands piqued Western curiosity about the world beyond Europe. While the great age of European voyages of discovery did not arrive until the 1400s, the Crusades nonetheless set the stage for the explorations of Christopher Columbus and other western European adventurers.

Similarly, the Crusades sparked European interest in commerce with other nations. These trade connections eventually helped bring about the historical period known as the Renaissance, which was a time of great enthusiasm for both trade

The Children's Crusade

One of the oddest—and saddest—tales from the Crusades involves the so-called Children's Crusade of 1212. Historians have long debated the specifics of this crusade, and some question whether it ever actually took place. In general terms, the Children's Crusade began when two young men named Stephen and Nicholas began encouraging young men and boys to travel to the Holy Land to fight for Christianity. As one chronicler described the event:

Many thousands of boys, ranging in age from six years to full maturity, left the plows or carts which they were driving, the flocks which they were pasturing, and anything else which they were doing. This they did despite the wishes of their parents, relatives, and friends who sought to make them draw back. . . . Thus, by groups of twenty, or fifty, or a hundred, they put up banners and began to journey to Jerusalem. . . . [They] were still of tender years and were neither strong enough nor powerful enough to do anything. Everyone, therefore, accounted them foolish and imprudent for trying

to do this. They briefly [explained] that they were equal to the Divine will in this matter and that, whatever God might wish to do with them, they would accept it willingly and with humble spirit. They thus made some little progress on their journey. Some were turned back at Metz, others at Piacenza, and others even at Rome. Still others got to Marseilles, but whether they crossed to the Holy Land or what their end was is uncertain. One thing is sure: that of the many thousands who rose up, only very few returned.

Quoted in James Brundage, *The Crusades: A Documentary Survey.* Milwaukee: Marquette University Press, 1962, p. 213.

An illustration shows the Children's Crusade of 1212. There are many questions about the specifics of this crusade and whether or not it actually took place.

and art among western Europeans. Moreover, although the Christians did not in the end defeat the Muslims in the Middle East, their victory over the Byzantines and the campaigns they did win against the Muslims raised Europe's estimation of its military might. In all these ways, the Crusades helped transform western Europe from the relatively unimportant backwater it was in 1000 to the much more influential power it became later in the millennium.

Today

The real legacy of the Crusades, however, lies in the relations between the Muslims and the Christians. The Crusades, of course, were only partly about religion. The evidence clearly indicates that political and economic considerations played a vital role in the fighting as well. In a purely religious conflict, no one would ever have suggested a wedding between Richard the Lionhearted's sister and Saladin's brother. The frequent alliances between Muslims and Christians that marked the Crusades would have been unthinkable. Christians would not have fought Christians during the Fourth Crusade, and Muslims would have been unified against the common Frankish enemy from the start. As Karabell wryly notes, "Religion mattered, ex-

cept when it didn't, and it didn't matter, except when it did."[72]

Still, there can be no denying that religious feeling helped make the Crusades what they were. "God wills it! God wills it!"[73] shouted the assembled knights and nobles after hearing Pope Urban's impassioned call to arms in 1095; according to a biographer, Saladin's "heart and mind were so taken over by this burning zeal for jihad [holy war] that he could speak of nothing else."[74] The religious aspect elevated the Crusades from being a mere struggle over land and money to something that seemed grander and more pure.

At the same time, it also caused tensions that still resound today. The Crusades helped to make possible a world in which some Muslims have become convinced that violence against the West is not only acceptable but also divinely inspired; a world in which some Christians have developed a deep-rooted fear and dislike of virtually all Muslims. The Crusades helped spawn an atmosphere of distrust on both sides, an us-against-them mentality that ignores the similarities between religions and cultures and stresses, instead, the differences. "On all sides," writes Karabell, "this lens distorts the past, constricts our present, and endangers our future."[75] Sadly, that is the most significant impact of the Crusades on the world today.

Notes

Chapter One: Europe and the Middle East

1. Quoted in Jonathan Phillips, *The Fourth Crusade and the Sack of Constantinople.* New York: Viking, 2004, p. 144.
2. Steven Runciman, *The First Crusade and the Foundation of the Kingdom of Jerusalem.* New York: Cambridge University Press, 1980, p. 50.
3. Michael Foss, *People of the First Crusade.* New York: Arcade, 1997, p. 21.
4. Runciman, *The First Crusade and the Foundation of the Kingdom of Jerusalem*, p. 49.
5. Quoted in Foss, *People of the First Crusade*, p. 22.
6. Quoted in Foss, *People of the First Crusade*, p. 33.

Chapter Two: The First Crusade

7. Quoted in David Willis McCullough, *Chronicles of the Barbarians.* New York: Times, 1998, p. 323.
8. Quoted in Foss, *People of the First Crusade*, p. 37.
9. Quoted in August C. Krey, *The First Crusade: The Accounts of Eye-Witnesses and Participants.* Gloucester, MA: Peter Smith, 1921, p. 29.
10. Quoted in Krey, *The First Crusade*, pp. 29–30.
11. Quoted in McCullough, *Chronicles of the Barbarians*, p. 324.
12. Foss, *People of the First Crusade*, p. 59.
13. Quoted in Foss, *People of the First Crusade*, p. 64.
14. Quoted in Krey, *The First Crusade*, p. 77.
15. Quoted in Foss, *People of the First Crusade*, p. 101.
16. Quoted in Foss, *People of the First Crusade*, p. 113.
17. Quoted in Foss, *People of the First Crusade*, p. 126.
18. Quoted in Krey, *The First Crusade*, p. 175.
19. Quoted in McCullough, *Chronicles of the Barbarians*, p. 333.
20. Quoted in McCullough, *Chronicles of the Barbarians*, p. 346.

Chapter Three: Holy Wars, Holy Warriors

21. Quoted in Krey, *The First Crusade*, p. 280.
22. Quoted in Foss, *People of the First Crusade*, p. 180.
23. Quoted in Krey, *The First Crusade*, pp. 280–81.
24. Quoted in Zachary Karabell, *Peace Be upon You: Fourteen Centuries of Muslim, Christian, and Jewish Coexistence.* New York: Alfred A. Knopf, 2007, p. 109.
25. Quoted in Internet Medieval Sourcebook, "William of Tyre: The Fall of

Edessa." www.fordham.edu/halsall /source/tyre-edessa.html.

26. Quoted in Jonathan Phillips, "War in Paradise," *History Today*, September 2007.

27. Quoted in Karabell, *Peace Be upon You*, p. 123.

28. Quoted in Karabell, *Peace Be upon You*, p. 125.

29. Quoted in Karabell, *Peace Be upon You*, p. 125.

30. Quoted in Internet Medieval Sourcebook, "The Battle of Hattin, 1187." www.fordham.edu/halsall/source /1187hattin.html.

31. Quoted in Internet Medieval Sourcebook, "The Battle of Hattin, 1187."

32. Quoted in Karabell, *Peace Be upon You*, p. 128.

33. Quoted in Geoffrey Hindley, *Saladin*. New York: Barnes & Noble, 1976, p. 2.

Chapter Four: Richard and Saladin

34. Quoted in Phillips, *The Fourth Crusade and the Sack of Constantinople*, p. 1.

35. Quoted in Geoffrey Regan, *Lionhearts: Saladin, Richard I, and the Era of the Third Crusade*. New York: Walker, 1999, p. 20.

36. Quoted in Lord John de Joinville, *Chronicles of the Crusades*. London: Henry G. Bohn, 1848, p. 88.

37. Hindley, *Saladin*, p. 142.

38. Quoted in Joinville, *Chronicles of the Crusades*, p. 88.

39. Quoted in Hindley, *Saladin*, p. 143.

40. Hindley, *Saladin*, p. 143.

41. Quoted in Hindley, *Saladin*, p. 158.

42. Quoted in Hindley, *Saladin*, p 160.

43. Quoted in Joinville, *Chronicles of the Crusades*, p. 216.

44. Regan, *Lionhearts*, p. 163.

45. Quoted in Regan, *Lionhearts*, p. 165.

46. Quoted in Hindley, *Saladin*, p. 178.

47. Quoted in Regan, *Lionhearts*, p. 209.

Chapter Five: The Fourth Crusade

48. Quoted in Phillips, *The Fourth Crusade and the Sack of Constantinople*, p. 6.

49. Quoted in John Clare Moore, *Pope Innocent III: To Root Up and to Plant*. Amsterdam: Brill, 2003, p. 105.

50. Quoted in Geoffrey de Villehardouin, *Memoirs*, trans. Frank T. Marzials, London: J.M. Dent, 1908, p 8.

51. Quoted in Phillips, *The Fourth Crusade and the Sack of Constantinople*, p. 107.

52. Quoted in Phillips, *The Fourth Crusade and the Sack of Constantinople*, p. 116.

53. Quoted in Margaret R.B. Shaw, ed., *Joinville and Villehardouin: Chronicles of the Crusades*. London: Penguin, 1963, p. 50.

54. Quoted in Villehardouin, *Memoirs*, p. 24.

55. Quoted in Phillips, *The Fourth Crusade and the Sack of Constantinople*, pp. 138–39.

56. Quoted in Shaw, *Joinville and Villehardouin*, p. 57.

57. Quoted in Villehardouin, *Memoirs*, p. 56.

58. Quoted in Phillips, *The Fourth Crusade and the Sack of Constantinople*, p. 244.

59. Quoted in Phillips, *The Fourth Crusade and the Sack of Constantinople*, p. 253.
60. Quoted in Phillips, *The Fourth Crusade and the Sack of Constantinople*, p. 259.
61. Quoted in Phillips, *The Fourth Crusade and the Sack of Constantinople*, p. 259.
62. Quoted in Morris Bishop, *The Middle Ages*. New York: Houghton Mifflin, 2002, p. 104.

Chapter Six: The End of an Era

63. Quoted in Ernest F. Henderson, trans., *Select Historical Documents of the Middle Ages*. London: George Bell and Sons, 1910, p. 341.
64. Quoted in Internet Medieval Sourcebook, "Frederick II's Crusade: Letters, 1229." www.fordham.edu/halsall/source/fred2cdelets.html.
65. Quoted in Internet Medieval Sourcebook, "Frederick II's Crusade: Letters, 1229."
66. Quoted in Internet Medieval Sourcebook, "The Capture of Jerusalem." www.fordham.edu/halsall/source/1144falljlem.html.
67. George Holmes, ed., *The Oxford Illustrated History of Medieval Europe.* New York: Oxford University Press, 1988, p. 259.
68. Bishop, *The Middle Ages*, p. 106.
69. Holmes, *The Oxford Illustrated History of Medieval Europe*, p. 259.
70. Bishop, *The Middle Ages*, p. 105.
71. Karabell, *Peace Be upon You*, p. 88.
72. Karabell, *Peace Be upon You*, p. 94.
73. Quoted in Phillips, *The Fourth Crusade and the Sack of Constantinople*, p. xviii.
74. Quoted in Karabell, *Peace Be upon You*, p. 122.
75. Karabell, *Peace Be upon You*, p. 5.

For Further Reading

Books

Morris Bishop, *The Middle Ages.* New York: Houghton Mifflin, 2002. A good one-volume history of the Middle Ages in Europe, including useful background information about the period and a clear description of the Crusades.

Samuel Willard Crompton, *The Third Crusade: Richard the Lionhearted vs. Saladin.* Philadelphia: Chelsea House, 2004. A well-written book focusing on Richard and Saladin. It includes information about the First and Second Crusades as well.

Katherine M. Doherty and Craig A. Doherty, *King Richard the Lionhearted and the Crusades in World History.* Berkeley Heights, NJ: Enslow, 2002. An account of the crusades and their importance, with particular emphasis on the Third Crusade and the experiences of Richard the Lionhearted.

James Harpur, *The Crusades: The Two Hundred Years War.* New York: Rosen, 2008. An overview of the crusades and the issues behind them.

Geoffrey Hindley, *Saladin.* New York: Barnes & Noble, 1976. An informative biography of the great Muslim leader Saladin. Well-researched and readable, it includes many interesting quotes by and about him.

Zachary Karabell, *Peace Be upon You: Fourteen Centuries of Muslim, Christian, and Jewish Coexistence.* New York: Alfred A. Knopf, 2007. A long but interesting look at how Muslims, Christians, and Jews have gotten along in the Middle East since the beginning of Islam. Karabell asserts that modern people tend to focus too much on the discord among the groups.

David Nicolle, *The Crusades and the Crusader States.* London: Osprey, 1988. As the title implies, this book gives information not only about the battles of the Crusades but also about the political and social situation in the Frankish Middle Eastern kingdoms. It also includes color illustrations.

Earle Rice Jr., *Life During the Crusades.* San Diego: Lucent, 1998. This book focuses on the lives of nobles, knights, and ordinary people during the period from 1000 to 1300.

Melanie Rice and Christopher Rice, *Crusades: The Struggle for the Holy Lands.* New York: Dorling Kindersley, 2001. A well-illustrated book that pictures artifacts from the Crusades. It provides information about the campaigns as well.

Steven Runciman, *A History of the Crusades: Volume 1: The First Crusade and the Foundation of the Kingdom of Jerusalem.* New York: Cambridge University Press, 1980. A thorough account of the First Crusade from both a military and a social perspective, written by one of the leading historians of the Crusades.

Other Resources

History Channel, *The Crusades.* DVD. Burlington, VT: A&E Home Video, 2005. A documentary on the Crusades.

Internet Medieval Sourcebook (www.fordham.edu/halsall/sbook.html). This Web site contains transcriptions and excerpts from first-person accounts pertaining to the Crusades. The site is endlessly fascinating, though the language of some of the translations is archaic and some of the documents are written in a complex, flowery style that can be difficult to interpret.

Index

Picture Credits

About the Author

Stephen Currie has written dozens of books for Lucent and other publishers, including several titles in Lucent's World History series. He is also a part-time teacher. He lives in New York State's Hudson Valley, where he enjoys bicycling, kayaking, and snowshoeing.